When the Meadowlark Sings

The Story of a Montana Family

When the Meadowlark Sings

The Story of a Montana Family

To Bev Vavrovsky

BEV VAVROVSKY
8865 E. BASELINE RD #507
MESA, AZ 85208-5300

Nedra Sterry

Nedra Sterry

RIVERBEND
PUBLISHING

1-24-04

Copyright 2003 by Nedra Sterry.
Published by Riverbend Publishing, Helena, Montana.

All rights reserved.

ISBN 1-931832-39-0
Cataloging-in-Publication Data on file at the Library of Congress.

Cover photo: Nedra Sterry, circa 1938
Design by DD Dowden, Helena, Montana.
Typeset in Sabon and Lucida
Manufactured in the United States of America.

03 04 05 06 07 08 09 10   CH   10 9 8 7 6 5 4 3 2 1

RIVERBEND PUBLISHING
P.O. Box 5883
Helena, MT 59604
1-866-787-2363
www.riverbendpublishing.com

To my mother, Adelia Frances Hanson

Acknowledgments

M any thanks to my family for their unflagging faith and support: To Rick, for the hours of editing and for his optimism and boundless enthusiasm; to Craig, for reading and editing and for his loving encouragement; to Alan, Sandra, and Jill for sharing the tears and the laughter; and to brother Bill for the memories.

A most grateful thank you to David McCumber, who took time from his busy life to read the manuscript and empowered me to believe I could write the book. To John Daniel, who gently but honestly showed me the way. To Chris Cauble and Martha Kohl for helping to put the manuscript into final form. To Pat Wallace, who listened, and to the "Ladies of the Club."

*"Without stories,
in some very real sense,
we do not know who we are or
who we might become."*

WILLIAM KITTREDGE, *Hole in the Sky*

Montana Map

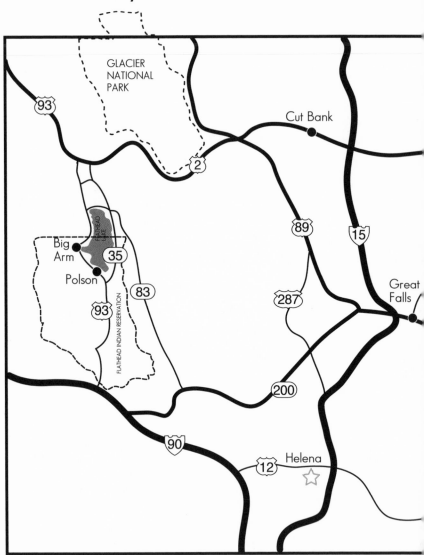

Map of schools and towns mentioned in *When the Meadowlark Sings*

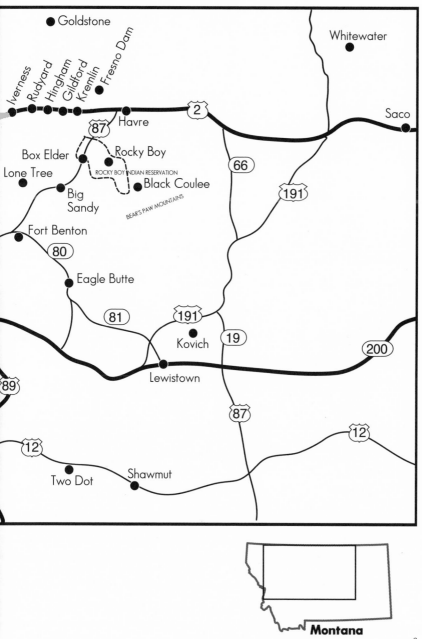

Goldstone

Whitewater

Iverness Rudyard Hingham Gildford Kremlin

Fresno Dam

2

Saco

87 Havre

Rocky Boy

Box Elder

66

Lone Tree

ROCKY BOY INDIAN RESERVATION

Black Coulee

191

Big Sandy

BEAR'S PAW MOUNTAINS

Fort Benton

80

Eagle Butte

81

191

Kovich

19

200

89

Lewistown

87

12

12

Two Dot

Shawmut

Montana

Autumn

I can still picture the rural Montana schools where Mama taught and where we lived. There was always the tiny, one-room teacher's quarters—the "teacherage"—a coal shed, two outhouses, and a white schoolhouse. Sometimes there was a set of swings with weathered wooden seats that left splinters in our bottoms. Although most of the schoolhouses sat on a treeless corner, fenced in with barbed wire and surrounded by miles of empty prairie, we were always anxious to explore. There were abandoned homestead shacks containing old magazines, bits of letters, and even clothing—dust-covered testimony of failed dreams. They held a great fascination for me. Who were these people? Where did they come from? Where did they go? Onto Washington or to the Oregon coast? Maybe they went back home to their relatives in the East. Once we found a big cardboard box with long skirts, ruffled blouses, and a fur-trimmed cape. No woman would leave without her best clothes. Maybe she died of flu or childbirth. There were no end of stories to be imagined.

We grew up in schoolhouses all across Montana. Nearly every year we moved to another school in a different part of the state. "Isn't this a lovely place, children?" my cheerful, optimistic mother would say. "This time I know we'll stay. I just feel it in my bones." But, as usual, we would burn up our winter's fuel allotment by Christmas. A single teacher would only have had to heat the teacherage at night, but we didn't all fit in the one-room dwelling. Instead, we four girls took turns sleeping with Mama, while our brother, Billy, and the other girls slept in the schoolhouse. We would put up a borrowed bed along with Billy's old army cot in the schoolhouse and make a fire. The school budget didn't include money for fuel for two fires, and by spring the school board members would be grumbling, and Mama would be looking for another teaching job.

"I know what we'll do next Saturday, children," Mama would say when the coal bin began to get low. "We'll have a picnic and fill our gunny sacks with buffalo chips on the way home." Of course, there hadn't been any buffalo roaming the prairie for many years. Mama knew that, but she thought it sounded better than "cow pies." We did a lot of walking and tried not to come home without a broken piece of fencepost or a branch from a dead cottonwood tree.

At each new school district we stopped at the local store in the nearest town to establish credit and buy our winter supplies. I remember the boxes of peaches and plums Mama brought home to can for the long winter months ahead and the baskets of concord grapes with their special pungent odor. We ate a lot of macaroni and cheese, but there would be dried apricots, apples, prunes, and raisins. Mama's raisin pie was a delectable treat. We would use up two hundred pound bags of flour and a huge bag of navy beans by spring.

Friday night we would sort and wash a big kettle of navy beans. If by some stroke of luck we had extra money, we'd have bacon rinds to cook with them. The beans were set on the back of the stove to soak while we all carried water to fill the tub and boiler for the weekly wash. We took turns at the washboard, the littlest kids scrubbing the socks as the white clothes bubbled on the stove. Saturday has always reminded me of the mingled smell of soapsuds, bean soup, bread baking, and wet wooden floors.

We all had our special jobs. Mine was washing the lantern and lamp chimneys, trimming the wicks, and filling the lamps. One of my clearest memories is the smell of Mama's Ponds cold cream as she cleaned her face at night and the acrid odor of the kerosene wicks as the lamps were blown out.

I enjoyed the winters as we snuggled down inside the schoolhouse while the storms howled around the buildings. One of the first things we did after filling our ticks with straw from the nearest straw stack was to pack straw around the base of the teacher's quarters and shovel dirt over that to keep the chill winds from blowing in. Then, after the first snowstorm, we would shovel snow over the dirt to keep the wind from blowing both the dirt and the straw away.

We watched while Mama set her yeast right after supper, and then before going to bed at night she'd stir in some flour. By morning it would be a bubbling pan of sponge. I can see her now, up to her elbows in flour and bread dough, eyeing the clock as she kneads and then covers it with a dishtowel. At noon she would pinch off handfuls of the risen dough, stretch it out thin, and fry it on top of the stove. We dipped it in a mixture of sugar and cinnamon and it was wonderful. Then she rolled the rest of the dough into loaves and it would be ready to bake by last recess. That was my sister Irene's job, keeping the fire just right, and taking the bread out of the oven to cool on a rack in time for supper.

Irene, the oldest, was small for her age, and she had other problems, too. Although she learned to read well, it took her longer than the rest of us. She never made it past the third-grade level, and when she was ten years old, Mama gave up and let her just sit and read in the classroom. I always thought of her as one of the little girls because she was small and she liked to play dolls with the little sisters. Betty Lou, the baby, stayed with the aunts in Minneapolis more than she stayed with us. She had chronic kidney trouble that affected her all of her life. Two years younger than I, Donna was the pretty one, with blue eyes and thick hair, and I always envied her. We were never close, not even after we grew up. Maribelle was four years older than I and ambitious. She planned to be a nurse from the time she was a little girl, and as soon as she was old enough she stayed in town, working for her room and board. Two years older than I, Billy was the only boy and my best buddy.

The first school I remember was the one at Eagle Butte, south east of Fort Benton, where Mama taught in 1920 and 1921. I clearly remember the barren, moonlike landscape covered with a fine lava rock and mica that glistened in the sunlight. We brought home chunks of mica to carve into shapes and hang in the win-

the windows to catch the sun. The Eagle Butte school district was a last resort for a teacher looking for a position. It had a bad reputation for truancy, and few teachers lasted out the term. It was already November when we arrived there. The last teacher, a young man, had left in October and we were just beginning to find out why.

On the first day of school the school board chairman looked Mama over. "Now we want you to learn these younguns somethin'," he said. "If they give you any trouble, you just beat 'em and we'll give 'em more of the same when they get home."

There were six first graders, about half of whom were probably under the legal age. You couldn't blame those mothers for wanting to get them out from under foot for a while, but it was tough on the teacher, especially when she had babies of her own. There were nearly twenty kids in that school, and the oldest boy was sixteen years old. Some of the boys had voices deeper than their fathers and were already shaving. They had been taken out of school for butchering, spring seeding, and hauling grain, and they were rarely ready for the eighth grade exams in the spring. They thought Mama would be an easy target. Mama was a small woman, five foot two, but I never saw the time when she wasn't in charge. She had blue eyes that never missed a thing, and she had most of the kids pretty much under control after the first week.

By noon the first day a half-dozen twenty-two shells had exploded in the pot-bellied stove, the crockery drinking fountain had been tipped over, and a bucket of coal had been spilled on the floor. The next morning when Mama tried to start the fire in the little cook stove in the teacherage, smoke began to pour into the room, and we all ran outside in our nightclothes coughing and choking. Mama lifted Billy onto the roof, and after a brief struggle he pulled balls of twine and snow from the chimney, and the smoke came billowing out.

"Don't any of you say anything about this," Mama told us during breakfast. "Not one word, even if they ask you. We'll just pretend nothing happened." But she had a plan.

The kids came to school the next day with bright eyes and expectant faces, but nothing changed except that Mama didn't read to us at noon, and recess time was cut in half. At four o'clock, the bell signaling the end of the school day was silent. Mama took the key to the schoolhouse out of her desk drawer, locked the door, and put the keys in her pocket. Then she went to the blackboard and wrote in big letters: "I HELPED STOP UP THE TEACHER'S CHIMNEY."

"When the guilty parties have all signed their names you may go home," she said. There were nervous giggles, whispers, and shuffling of feet, and the clock ticked on. Finally one of the big boys stood up. "If we ain't home to do the chores my Pa'll be mad and you'll get fired."

Mama jingled the keys. "We'll see," she said, and waited— and waited, until all but the smallest boys had signed their names. When at last the sound of a wagon was heard and an irate father pounded on the door, Mama unlocked it and let him in. Before he could say a word, she pointed to the blackboard. He looked, he read, and then burst into a booming laugh.

"By golly," he bellowed. "I tink we got us a teacher dis time." Mama had gambled and won. There were other tries at getting rid of the teacher, but they were half-hearted and only to keep in practice.

Before Eagle Butte

I am trying to think back to a time when Mama might have had a normal happy life. I don't think she ever did. She just made the best of things. "Tell us about the olden days, Mama," we would beg, and the stories she told were not happy ones.

Mama was only four, one of ten children in Madelia, Minnesota, when her mother died of a stroke at the age of forty-seven in 1887. The younger children were taken into various homes around the community. She remembered her father as a dour and surly man she rarely saw. The family that took my mother wasted very little affection on the small orphan. Their only child, a boy, teased and tormented Mama unmercifully, and she was often punished for things he had done. They told Mama outrageous stories about the Indian massacre that had taken place in Mankato thirty years before and threatened to let the Indians have her if she didn't carry out her tasks to their satisfaction.

She was doing the work of a grown woman by the time she was ten. She carried the water for the family baths and weekly washing, helped cook the meals, and washed the dishes when supper was over. They gave her fifty cents a week, and she would need every cent of it to pay for teacher's college when she was old enough. When she was fourteen she answered an ad in the Mankato paper placed by a family with six children who needed her as much as she needed them. She worked there until, at the age of seventeen, she began teacher's college in Mankato. Working part time she earned her teacher's certificate and set off on her own.

She rolled her hair into a bun and borrowed a pair of pince-nez glasses in an effort to look older when she had her picture taken and then started applying for a teacher's position. She was told over and over that she was too young, and was almost ready to despair when she was hired to teach in the Hanson school district. That school was considered undesirable because the teacher had to board with the Hanson family and share a room with one of the three sisters. By that time Mama wasn't too choosy, so she accepted the position, and the die was cast.

It was there that she met my father, the youngest of five siblings. Although his sisters told my mother that Will was spoiled, selfish, and had a nasty temper, she fell in love, and they were engaged by Christmastime.

Will and his older brother Fred brought home pamphlets about the rich land in Montana that could be had for the taking. They decided to marry their sweethearts and seek their fortunes. In 1912 they found land north of Fort Benton, Montana, filed and began to build their homestead shanties. It was hard, grinding work breaking and planting the new prairie land, but in some places the crops grew so high that only the men's heads and the top of the women's hats showed above the burgeoning wheat.

In the first good years my parents borrowed money from the bank and planned to build a house and barn when the wheat was harvested and sold. After all, the land was new, the wheat grew tall and lush, and there was promise of better things to come. The next spring they plowed and seeded the fields, their optimism boundless. Then came long weeks of sun and soft winds, and the wheat grew tall and bountiful again. In another week, harvest would begin, the threshing crews were spoken for, and all was in readiness.

Uncle Fred and Aunt Ella had decided to wait to build their house, and that turned out to be the right decision. The black clouds came bringing hail that second year. Then the merciless sun and hot winds finished what was left. Grasshoppers, drought, and other pestilence followed the next few years, and the grim-faced bankers finished the dream.

One farm can be totally wiped out by hail while another farm three miles away can survive untouched, and so it was that my Uncle Fred became the owner of my parents' homestead in 1914, for hail is a capricious thing. My father worked then for other farmers more fortunate than he had been. Luckily my mother had her teacher's certificate, and the country school was just two miles from the homestead. The school needed a teacher, and she got the job. With Mama teaching, Mama and Papa continued to live in their house on the homestead until they moved to Fort Benton the fall of 1916.

Before they moved, Papa found work with a transient threshing crew. He went to town one day with a wagonload of wheat that had been gleaned and thrashed, which he planned to sell to buy provisions to last while he was away. It was all that was left from the ruined fields. When he didn't get home in time for supper that night, Mama walked the floor and worried, finally getting to sleep at first light. The sound of a motor in the yard awakened her. The sun was high in the sky already, and she hurried to dress. When she went outside, there was Will, wearing a black leather helmet and boots, spinning around the yard, sending up a hail of pebbles and a cloud of dust. He had sold the team and wagon to buy a shiny black motorcycle and sidecar. Mama cried that day, but Will was like a child, admiring the way the handlebars caught the sunlight.

"I'll be able to come home more often now," he said, smiling the boyish smile that had won her heart.

"Oh, Will." She covered her face with her hands, trying to stop the tears, and then hopelessly turned her back and started for the house.

"Come on, get in and I'll take you for a ride." She shook her head.

"For Christ sake, what are you bawling about?" He jumped off the machine and ran after her. "Come on, Deely. Come on, now," he wheedled. "You know I need transportation. Come and look at the groceries I got you. The storage compartment is full of stuff for you and the kids." Irene and Maribelle were up now, circling and admiring the shiny machine.

"You know a good thing when you see it, don't you, my pretty little girls? Come here and Papa will take you both for a spin."

He buckled them into the sidecar in spite of Mama's protests and tore up the road and over the hill. Climbing on the hitching post, she could barely see them in the cloud of dust going past the schoolhouse and up the road toward Uncle Fred's place. It was much later when he returned.

"I had to take her over to show old mealy-mouth Fred," he said. "Boy, was he jealous." Then, unbuckling the girls, he unloaded the groceries.

"What have you got for breakfast, woman?" he asked.

After they left the farm the family lived in Fort Benton in a small rented house. Mama was "expecting" again, this time with my brother, the only one of the children to be born in a hospital. Mama had a kerosene incubator in the cellar and went down early one morning to turn the eggs. She tripped on the hem of her bathrobe and dropped the lantern, starting a fire. Ripping off her robe she beat out the flames, but by this time her nightgown was on fire. She raced up the stairs, grabbed a blanket, pulled it around herself, and ran outside, rolling on the ground. Luckily Papa was still there, and he roused the neighbors to watch the girls and help him get Mama to the hospital. My brother, Billy, was born there and was a healthy baby in spite of the trauma. Mama was badly burned and carried dreadful scars from chest to thigh for the rest of her life.

The family stayed in Fort Benton for four years. I was two years old when Mama, my sisters, my brother, and I left for Eagle Butte, and Papa went with a threshing crew looking for work elsewhere. We didn't see him so often after that. He would come to visit us once in a while, roaring up on his motorcycle with candy and presents and tall tales, but I didn't like him. I remember the arguments and Papa's loud voice, and I was always glad when he went away again.

Trains

The summer of 1922 we lived in Big Sandy, a small town between Great Falls and Havre, while we waited for school to start in mid-October at the nearby Lone Tree School. Big Sandy remains vivid in my mind. It is where I gained the thick, white scar still visible on the heel of my left hand.

The day I received the wound that gave me that scar, Mama was in bed. She never stayed in bed, so I thought she was sick. The neighbor lady was there, and she told Maribelle to take us kids down to the station to see the circus train.

"And don't bring them back until someone comes to get you," she said. "This shouldn't take too long."

Maribelle was shepherding us even though Irene was the oldest. Irene never got to be the boss because she ran away sometimes, and we all had to watch out for her. I was four that summer and didn't like being bossed by anyone. The sky was a vibrant blue, and we could smell the smoke from the train as it sat on the track. I ran ahead when I saw that some of the doors to the circus cars were open even though I could hear Maribelle yelling for me to wait.

There were bars across the doors of the railroad cars, but a darling little monkey was reaching through them. He was so cute I thought he wanted to shake hands with me. Instead he grabbed my hand and in a flash bit it clear to the bone. I remember the metallic taste of blood, the screams, and the pain. "Take her home," someone said, and someone else said, "No, you can't take her home, her mother is having a—." A third voice said, "Shush," and I watched the blood soaking my dress and screamed, "Mama, Mama." Remembering this, I can still smell the Lysol and see the cloudy water turning red.

A large lady with hairs growing out of a wart in her chin tore strips from a dishtowel and bandaged my hand. "You poor children," she kept saying. "You poor, poor children." When we were allowed to go home, there was a new little baby in bed with Mama. "This is your little sister Betty Lou," Mama said.

That summer a boxcar overturned on the railroad tracks. It was loaded with Easter eggs that scattered on the ground. Kids from all over town filled their pockets. I filled my skirt and we ate and ate those candy eggs, finally just licking out the marshmallow centers. I guess that's why I still don't like the taste of vanilla.

The very best memory of that summer in Big Sandy was the time Mama sent me to the neighbors to borrow some coffee, and when I smell freshly ground coffee, I think of that sunny morning. When the lady let me in the door, I gasped with delight as I stepped into a kitchen filled with dancing rainbows. It was the prettiest kitchen I had ever seen, and when she saw how enthralled I was, she took me by the hand and led me over to the window. "This is a prism," she said, "and when the sun hits it just right, this is what happens." And then she let me hold it. I thanked her and went home, but I knew I had been given much more than coffee. I watch the rainbows dancing on my ceiling today and feel like a little girl again.

Not long after a young couple came to stay with the neighbors next door. The lady came often to visit with Mama. One day I heard her crying, so I stood by the door and listened. She said she couldn't have babies, and her husband was talking about divorce. She brought him to see the new baby Betty Lou. "Why do we have to fool around with diapers and sleepless nights," he said, "when we could have a cute one like her?" Then he picked me up and swung me around.

The lady came over to our house every day. She asked if she could take me downtown shopping. She bought me an ice cream cone and took me home with her and curled my hair. I liked the lady. She felt soft and smelled nice when she hugged me. Once when she came over to visit with Mama, I was reading the funny papers, and she laughed. "Look, she's pretending she can read that."

"She can," Mama said.

"But she's only four years old," the lady said as she gave me a squeeze.

"Bob has to see this." She ran home and came back with her husband. She told me to read the *Katzenjammer Kids* to him, and then they both laughed and told me I was smart. One day she took me to the Big Store and bought me a red dress and brand new patent leather shoes. I had never had new shoes before. You only went to the Big Store if you had a lot of money. You could buy eggs and potatoes and overshoes and underwear and lots of other things. Mama never went there.

One night Mama packed a little suitcase with my new clothes. She put her arms around me and cried and then she rocked me to sleep. I can only remember snippets after that. Nothing really connects. I do remember the lady saying that I was to call her Mama. I knew that saying it wouldn't make it so, so I decided to play make believe and not mean it.

Why was I going away from Mama? My stomach felt like a fist, but I swallowed hard and didn't cry in my new red dress and shiny shoes. Then I was on a train in a sleeping car. My clothes were in a green mesh bag on the wall above the little bed. I felt the swaying of the train and listened to the clicking wheels. The next morning I was walking in the train to the dining car with the pretty lady and the tall man with curly black hair. He said, "You're going to spoil our little girl, Mary, before we even get her home." He picked me up and tickled me until I was out of breath.

I remember the man's rough whiskers, the lady crying, and loud angry words. Then I was on a train again. This time I was not sleeping in a little bed with my clothes in a basket over my head. This time I was sitting in a hard seat and traveling with a grouchy woman who smelled of tobacco smoke and garlic. She hardly spoke to me, but I didn't care. I was going home to Mama.

It was night, and a young girl was waiting at the train depot. She told me that she was the hired girl for the school board chairman's wife and would take me home to Mama in the morning. I snuggled up to her generous bosom, but I hardly slept at all. I was so excited about seeing my family again. We had breakfast while it was still dark. Then, just as the sun came up, we started off in the buggy. The wind was cold. The girl lashed the horse, and her long hair streamed behind her as we tore along the rocky prairie road.

She couldn't go too fast for me.

Sweetheart

Harvest was in full swing when Mama decided to go back to Eagle Butte and get our things herself. The rent was due on the house in Big Sandy, and she wanted to get settled in before school started. Some of the school board members had promised to have the moving job done but had put it off, and now they were all too busy. "All I need is the loan of a team and wagon," she said. "You will all be busy shocking the wheat, and we'll be back long before you need them."

Everyone but the littlest kids worked in the field during harvest. We had always helped with this part of the harvest when we were asked, and I enjoyed how important I felt when I was allowed to help. I remember the fragrance of the newly cut wheat and the shattering sun on our backs. To my best recollection, this was how it was done. We picked up two sheaves of wheat, balancing them on their flat bottoms like a tepee, then two more, slapping them together for the hayracks to pick up. We would have tiny slivers of straw in our arms and legs when we were through. We girls wore dresses, of course, so we had more slivers than the boys. It would be days before they festered and we could get all of them out.

Lars and Jens were earnestly trying to talk Mama out of going without a man to help. "Yah, you got to be real careful fordin' that river," Jens told her. "That ain't no job for a woman. She's pretty low now, though, what with no rain this summer." Lars nodded his head. "You better wait another week. Low or high, she's a devil to cross."

"I've driven a team of horses," Mama said, shaking the dust from her skirts. "Yes, and I have forded a river, too. I'm sure we'll be fine. Now let's go look at that team. I want to get started early in the morning."

She came out of the barn looking pale. "My heavens," she said. "It's a mule and a horse. Will they work together?"

"Yep . . . name's Bob, the horse that is. Now that beauty there, name's Sweetheart, and there ain't an animal in the county more deserving of the name."

Mama blanched and then lifted her chin. "Well then," she said, "I guess I had better start getting acquainted with . . . uh . . . Sweetheart."

The next morning they all gathered around as Sweetheart and Bob started out of the yard.

"Oh wait." Jens was smiling. "I forgot to tell you. She does get a little stubborn sometimes. If she does, the best way to get her moving again is holler her name good and loud, and maybe swear at her a little bit." Martha Olson whispered in Mama's ear and then hugged her and laughed as she helped her into the wagon.

They loaned Mama a tarp to cover our household goods, and Martha Olson hugged her again. "You just leave the little ones with me, and I promise that they will be as safe as my own."

This time I would rather have stayed behind and helped shock wheat. Those Norwegian women were great cooks and did their best to outdo each other with the lunches they served. I thought of the platters of fried chicken, bowls of potato salad, and the wonderful pies, and my mouth began to water. But Mama said no, so off I went.

Mama packed a big lunch and took blankets along for us to sit on, and it was a beautiful day with no clouds in the sky. She thought we might get back by suppertime, but the team was tired, and she didn't want to stir up any bad feelings between herself and Sweetheart. As always, Mama turned the trip into a family outing, and we sang most of the way.

We were almost to the river by noon. Mama had said we would picnic there in the shade of the trees, but then the sun slipped behind a cloud and a wind came up. The trees along the bank of the river were changing color. Leaves were beginning to blow into the water, and the sky was slate gray now with the wind stronger and cooling fast. We were looking forward to getting out of the wagon and running around, but Mama decided we had better eat our lunch on the way. The horse snorted and almost jerked the reins out of Mama's hands when she started driving across the ford. Although the river was quite low and only about forty feet across, the noise spooked the horse so she had to use the whip.

"Bob," she yelled, "you there, Bob," but he just shook his head and snorted. Sweetheart finally bent her neck and started across, so Bob had to go along.

"I'm hungry," Irene grumbled. "And I gotta go." Billy and I agreed that it was time to eat, so despite Mama's worry about the change in the weather, she pulled the wagon off the road. More clouds were gathering and the wind was colder now. The team needed to be fed and watered and given a rest, or Mama never would have stopped. We gave them half of the oats we had brought along and then got on the road again.

What had begun as an adventure was fast becoming an endurance test. Without any warning, the sky opened up and it started to rain. Mama drove the team under some trees, and we dragged out the tarp and spread it over us. Mama got soaked and the animals were getting balky again. The roads were becoming slick, and the wheels gathered mud, making it harder for the team to pull the wagon. At last we could see the schoolhouse in the distance. We never thought we would be happy to see that place again, but we were glad of the shelter when we finally stabled and fed the team and got inside ourselves.

Irene and Billy brought in some wood from the shed, and we got a fire going. We ate the rest of our picnic lunch, saving some apples for breakfast, and made beds on the floor. We went to sleep to the music of rain on the roof, a sound the farmers had waited for all summer. The floor got pretty hard by morning, but when we woke up the rain had stopped. There were puddles in the yard, and it was messy getting our things transferred to the wagon. We all helped. I got the small boxes and the lighter loads. We watered and fed the team and were soon on our way.

The mud was a sticky gumbo now that built up in the wagon spokes, so it was slow going. We had to stop and scrape the gumbo from the spokes almost every mile. When we reached the river it was plain to see that it had risen, and the water was running faster. The team approached the edge of the ford and stopped. Mama yelled and cracked the whip, and still they wouldn't move into the river. "Sweetheart," she yelled. "Come on you kids, yell!" We all hollered, "Sweetheart, get going there," but old Bob was trying to head upstream, and the water was up to the hubs now. I could imagine that cold muddy water closing over our heads, and I was scared. We were flatlanders, and none of us could swim.

"All right then, Sweetheart, you son-of-a-bitch!" Mama yelled, and that mule laid its ears back against its head. Its eyes rolled, and it pulled ahead, dragging Bob along to the riverbank and plunging and heaving up the other side. We all looked at each other with astonishment. We had never heard Mama swear before. She climbed down from the wagon and walked around in front of the team, her hair loose from its knot and her skirt wet and muddy. Tears were running down her face as she patted Sweetheart on the nose and told her she was the best damn horse in the country.

We made it back to the Olson's before dark, and the whole family was out in the yard to greet us. Martha and Mama looked at each other and smiled. "I guess you used the magic word," Martha said, and Mama laughed.

We were all settled in a few days, and Mama had the respect of the entire community of Lone Tree that year.

Wooza

Mama had stood her ground in 1925 and was the first teacher in years to make it through the term in Whitewater, a small town north of Glasgow, and—wonderful news—she had been asked to come back the following year. The kids still tried her patience, although she had to laugh sometimes at their schemes. One involved Horst Strindmo, a bachelor farmer in the community whose hopes rose anew each time a new lady teacher arrived. The homeliest man I have ever seen, with a build like the Neanderthal man in the *National Geographic,* he was determined to find someone to share his life, and he set his sights on Mama. Some of the big kids decided to encourage his ardor. Mama had earned their grudging respect, but this was just too good an opportunity to miss. They sent him valentines and signed her name and left love notes in his mailbox.

One night there was a mighty knock on the door, and there stood Horst with a sack of candy in one hand and a gunnysack in the other. He gave the candy to my little sister and tossed the gunnysack on the floor. Suddenly it began to jerk and flop. Pandemonium broke loose. We girls shrieked and jumped on the bed for safety as Horst untied the string.

"See," he said, "I bring chicken wooza for Mrs. Lady." Feathers flew as the frightened chicken darted around the room, squawking and beating its wings, until Horst caught it. "You cook him," he said. "And I come for supper tomorrow night. We talk den. You don't worry, Mrs. Lady, I like many kids." He handed the chicken to my mother, who just shook her head.

"But it's alive," she said, "And I don't have a hatchet."

"Oh, I fix." Horst grabbed the chicken and with one quick snap of the wrist wrung its neck. The poor thing was still flopping as Horst handed it to Mama. "Tank you for da walentines, Mrs. Lady," he said, and went out the door, his ears burning. My brother said he heard the sound of running feet and stifled giggles when Horst stepped outside.

The next morning the school kids were rolling their eyes and smirking. "Did you have company last night, Mrs. Hanson?" one of the big kids asked. Mama just looked at him. "Take out your books," she said. "We are going to have a test."

Sure enough, Horst did come for dinner that night, resplendent in a rusty old suit and smelling of mothballs. Mama's dumplings would melt in your mouth, and Horst lost no time in making his intentions clear. He needed a wife and housekeeper, and she needed a man to take care of her and the children. Mama was nearly at a loss for words, but she thanked him and said she already had a husband, although he was not with us now. She did agree that he probably needed a housekeeper, and she needed a summer job. If he and the hired man would clean out one of the empty granaries for a bunkhouse, we would work for our room and board for the summer. Horst turned red and his moustache twitched, and then he turned pale, but after studying Mama for a minute he said, "We can try it out and see how it works."

Mama went to bed that night without a worry for our immediate future at least. It never dawned on us kids how much she dreaded the end of the school term. She had to find work and keep us children fed, so while we looked forward to the excitement of packing up and moving on, she was close to despair sometimes. That summer turned out to be one of the best ever, and Horst became a good and generous friend to us all.

It was there that I found an ad in a farm magazine. "Sell six subscriptions and this cuddly suck-a-thumb dolly will be yours," it said. Although I was nearly eight years old, I had never had a doll of my own, and I fiercely desired this one. I walked miles that summer and collected hoarded money from farmer's wives who really didn't have it to spend but couldn't resist my pleading. When all the subscriptions were sold I settled down to wait. Did I say settled? I was a whirlwind of motion, haunting the mailbox a half-mile away.

If I saw three white horses, my package would be there. If I found more than ten eggs in the chicken coup or could recite five lines from *Hiawatha*, it would surely be in the mailbox that day. When at last the package did arrive, I walked up to the house with the others trailing me and into the bedroom, where I put it unopened on the closet shelf.

I remained unmoved by the pleas of my sisters and in fact did not open the package until noon the next day. The doll was much smaller than I had imagined it, and it was made of pink sticky rubbery material that smelled like mice. It did have a hole in its face where the thumb could be, and one in its bottom. Just like a real baby, the ad had said. I played with it for about fifteen minutes and then turned it over to my sisters and never touched it again. I learned something that summer that stayed with me all my life. The joy of anticipation far outweighs the possibilities of disappointment. That became my philosophy anyway, and it has helped me through some bad times.

We ate carrots, turnips, peas, and potatoes right out of the garden all summer. We helped Mama can peas and beans and corn enough for Horst and for our family, too. Billy was working for the Sand brothers, a pair of bachelors a few miles away, and I thought it would be a relief not to have him bossing me all the time, but I missed him. We raised a hundred chicks, and I didn't think we would ever get tired of fried chicken, but we did. One day Mama asked Horst if he could bring some red meat the next time he went to town. He looked shocked that she would ask but didn't say anything.

A week later he came home with a big slab of red meat. Mama fixed a roast ringed with vegetables, and it smelled delicious. We were always hungry and could hardly wait for supper. As we were sitting down to the table, Mama said, "Should I can some of this meat Mr. Strindmo? It will surely spoil before we can eat it all."

"Do you like dat meat, Mrs. Lady?" he asked.

"Of course I do," she said.

"Dat's hor-r-rse meat." Horst and the hired man laughed uproariously as she turned pale and hurried into the kitchen, followed by us kids.

They finished off the rest of the roast all by themselves. We learned that there were a lot of ways to cook chicken and enjoyed every morsel of it the rest of the summer.

A farm can be a dangerous place for kids, and especially daredevils like we were. We sprained many ankles jumping off the chicken coop and stepped on a lot of nails. Mama always had a bottle of Lysol disinfectant around, and coupled with a big jar of Mentholatum, I believe it was the only medicine we ever used.

There was a big hopper in the barn with a handle on the side. It was used to treat seed wheat in the spring, and I always gave it a turn whenever I walked by. Once I lifted the cover to watch the paddle as I turned the handle. Within minutes I was feeling nauseated and started running for the house. I never made it. Mama happened to be looking out the window and saw me fall. Luckily Horst had just come in for lunch, and I was taken to a doctor in town. The dust in that bin was a deadly poison, meant for killing insect eggs and noxious weeds, and it nearly killed me.

When I woke up four days later, beautiful white curtains were blowing across my face, and I thought they were angel wings. Mama was sitting beside me and burst into tears when I spoke to her. Two days later we were on our way back to the farm. I was kept in bed for a while but soon started getting my strength back.

While I was drinking the broth she brought me one day, I told Mama that I was going to have white curtains on my windows when I grew up just like the ones at the doctor's house in Whitewater. She gave me a strange look. "There weren't any curtains on those windows. I was there the whole time, and the windows were bare."

I knew Mama wouldn't lie, but she could be mistaken. I saw them and felt them on my face.

Porky

It was the fall of 1928, and we had two glorious months to roam after school and on Saturdays. My brother and I went on long walks every day. Our special place was the rim rocks about a mile from the Pleasant Valley School near Shawmut. They were beautiful and almost perpendicular, with dark orange and pale pink shale and rocks slashed by shades of brown. They formed a sort of crescent, almost a small grand canyon. Footing was precarious at best, but we knew all the hand and footholds.

Below the rim rock walls, slender green willows grew beside a lovely sparkling stream that flowed into a small pool. Long thick grasses grew there, and we got the idea of cutting the willows out of a circle and then weaving the remaining young willows with grass to make a shelter as high as our heads. I've often wondered if the willows could have kept growing to make a tent-sized shelter for a weary traveler.

It was a personal Eden and a great place to explore. There were arrowheads made of agate, and we found petroglyphs on a large flat rock. It had stick figures and what looked like antelope and buffalo, and young as I was I felt a sense of awe in that place. We enlisted the other kids and became an Indian tribe and called ourselves the Arrowheads. Billy was the chief, of course. He taught us how to walk like Indians with our toes pointed straight ahead.

Once, climbing back up the cliff, we poked a porcupine from behind a bush, and the next day Billy showed me a book he had been reading about survival in the wilderness. Porcupine, it declared, had saved many lives and even tasted a little bit like pork.

"Mama," Billy said that evening, "it says in this book that porcupine is good to eat. If we catch one and skin it, will you cook it for us?"

Mama smiled. "Now Billy, you know perfectly well that you can't catch a porcupine without getting any needles in you, so don't even think about it."

"Yeah, but if we do catch one, will you cook it?"

"Maybe," Mama said.

The next morning Billy showed me a six-foot long stick, another stick with a forked end, and a ball of binder twine. "I've got the perfect plan," he said to me. "Let's go get that porcupine." Mama should never have told him it wasn't possible. She looked a little worried as we set out that morning.

I was getting a bit uneasy about the adventure myself, but as usual I followed along while Billy explained to me how it could be done. He cut off a piece of the twine and fashioned a slipknot at one end, repeating it with another piece of twine. He would, he said, "get the critter on its back," and while he held it down with the forked stick I was to neatly drop the slipknot over one back foot and jerk it tight. Then I was to hold the stick while he made another slipknot and captured the other back leg. We would repeat this procedure on the front legs, slip the long pole through the twine and carry the porcupine hanging upside down as we scrambled for handholds back up the cliff. It seemed perfectly plausible, as all of Billy's schemes did, and so we set off, planning on roast porcupine that night.

Unfortunately, the little creature had plans of its own. We looked all over that little valley and almost gave up before we finally found him. Billy poked him out of his hiding place and onto his back. I got the first slipknot over one of his hind feet, and then he got away, trailing the length of twine, and into a little cave in the side of the cliff. We pulled and yanked on the twine, but he wouldn't budge. We lit a fire and made a smudge of grass at the opening of his cave, but still he wouldn't leave his shelter. When Billy finally poked him out, the battle of wills continued. What we had planned would only take about an hour took us all afternoon.

We got him at last and started up the cliff. We both took an end of the pole, and the porcupine hung between us as we reached for hand and footholds up that cliff, trying not to let him slide too close to either side. It was treacherous and exhausting, and I begged Billy to give up and let the poor thing go, but he had his mind set on roast porcupine, maybe with an apple in its mouth, so we forged ahead. The sun was just setting as we came trudging up the road to the schoolhouse with a bristly ball of needles swinging between us.

Mama's face turned pale when she opened the door and saw us with our prize. She pulled herself together, though, and thought fast. Billy was already sharpening the knife when she told him that we would have to wait until morning to butcher the animal. "Besides," she said, "I've fixed spaghetti, your favorite supper. We would have to stay up until midnight to cook him. No, we'll wait until morning."

Billy was reluctant to delay his plans but finally agreed. We tied the little animal to a steel bolt in the manger, and the next morning we were up early, racing each other to the barn. It was empty. Only a ragged length of chewed twine was left, and there was a hole in the corner with claw marks in the earth floor. I privately thought some of the marks looked like they could have been made with a coal shovel. We didn't ask, and Mama didn't say. Billy was ready to start the hunting expedition all over again, right after breakfast, but Mama said, "The new Sears catalog came yesterday, Billy, and the air rifle you want is still there. Let's go look." I think "Porky" found new campgrounds after his narrow escape. Anyway we never saw him again.

Needles

There were five families in the Lincoln school district, near Shawmut, where Mama taught in 1925: a widow with a fourteen-year-old daughter; the Benbow family, with a nine-year-old son and twelve-year-old daughter; three Bakers, three Larsons, and four of us Hansons. Maribelle, who had skipped several grades, had gone to live in Shawmut, where she worked for her board and attended high school. That was a terrible winter for all of us, and we were lucky to survive. I remember only gray cold cloudy days and the smell of coal smoke when I think of that place.

Today a phone call brings parents to school to pick up a sick child, but it wasn't so easy in a country school in 1925. It was November, and the darkening sky contributed to the cheerlessness of the schoolhouse and the children bent over their books. When one of the little boys complained of a headache and sore throat, Mama put the eighth-grade girl in charge, wrapped herself and the boy up, and started out across the prairie toward the boy's farm. The boy, Howard Benbow, and his sister, Mary, both had dark curly hair and were always the first to raise their hands when Mama asked the class a question. Mama said they were extremely bright. I remember them especially because they had both sets of grandparents living with them, and I thought that would be wonderful.

We watched as Mama and Howard disappeared in the sifting snow. A full-fledged storm was blowing in when Howard's father brought Mama home on his way to town to get the doctor. Snow had covered the schoolhouse steps by early afternoon when the county nurse confirmed the doctor's suspicion of diphtheria and declared a quarantine on the community. The nurse traveled to school and inoculated all of the children before they were sent home. The vaccine was too late for Mama. She was already infected.

Diphtheria is a disease that moves swiftly, forming a large membrane in the throat of its victim. In those days, either coughing dislodged the membrane and the patient recovered, or the patient suffocated. Nothing could be done for Mama in the hospital that couldn't be done at home, so despite her young age, Maribelle returned to the teacherage to care for her and for us children.

The doctor drove the fourteen-mile round trip every few days to check on Mama. He was an old country doctor, who had refused to trade his horse and buggy in for a car, although cars were already fairly common. "My old horse will take me home if I drift off on one of my midnight calls, and I can't depend on a tin Lizzie to do that," he often said. When he came to visit Mama, he sometimes brought the county nurse with him. She was a jolly, sweet-faced woman who always had a joke for us, and she helped Maribelle bathe Mama and tidy the teacherage before she left. We were always glad to see her.

Maribelle was as competent as a much older person. She cooked our meals and brought them over to the schoolhouse. We ate a lot of macaroni and boiled potatoes and bean soup. She would set the pans on the doorstep and run back inside, just in case the needles hadn't done their job and we could still catch the deadly germs from her.

On one of his visits, the doctor told us that the little Benbow boy had died, and his grandmother had died of a stroke while preparing him for his burial. I don't know how it happened that we were allowed to attend the funeral when we had been quarantined for three weeks, but we were. It made a big impression on me: The small casket carried by the uncles, followed by the bigger one, both interred on the same day. The whole community was there. Someone played "In the Sweet Bye and Bye" on the violin. It was the saddest sound I ever heard.

We had read almost every book in the school library before the doctor announced that the membrane had come loose from Mama's throat and that she would recover. We were jubilant, but then, two days later, he told us that Maribelle had come down with the disease and was very sick. He made the trip out from town every day now because she was gravely ill and he had become fond of this plucky little girl who had taken on the responsibility of caring for her mother. We all gave thanks when the doctor told us that Maribelle was getting better.

There were eight other cases of diphtheria in the community, but they all survived. Before school reopened, we fumigated the premises. It was tedious work, standing all the books on end and propping them open. The smell of formaldehyde lingered for days after the canisters had burned out, and I remember how awful it smelled. We couldn't possibly stay in the schoolhouse and breathe those strong fumes. We had to air the schoolhouse out for three nights, so that meant doubling up in the one-room teacherage on the one bed and Billy's cot. Mama slept on Billy's army cot, and she made him a bed on the floor. Donna, Irene, Bette, and I slept crossways on the bed and did a lot of whining and complaining and kicking each other. Maribelle had gone back to her family in Shawmut. She was as thin as a ghost but had kept up her studies, and her grades hadn't suffered.

We were living at another school near Shawmut three years later when Maribelle was brought home from town with scarlet fever, the only case reported in the county. It meant another school closing, but this was a common occurrence in those years, and it was back to the schoolhouse for us while Mama now nursed Maribelle. The scarlet fever became as bad as the diphtheria had been. Maribelle was very sick, but Mama didn't get it this time, and it looked as if none of the rest of us were going to get it, either.

If parents had been suspicious at first of the shots the county nurse recommended, they began to believe that vaccinations saved lives. We had them all, the painful ugly smallpox blisters that swelled up and itched and formed nasty scabs and, worse, the shots from long needles to prevent scarlet fever, measles, and, eventually, even the deadly infantile paralysis. Meanwhile, we stayed in the schoolhouse, carrying on the same routine, with

Mama bringing our meals over and setting them on the porch. Billy and I were responsible for keeping the fire going in the furnace, and we soon burned up all the good coal, so there was nothing but slack left in the coal bin. It burned, but produced an oily smoke that left a coating on everything it touched.

When the quarantine was over we looked like raccoons. We were covered with soot, our eyes and nostrils looking as though they had been ringed with black color crayon. We carried water and filled the boiler and then took turns washing our bodies and greasy hair. Then it was back to the fumigating exercise, followed by scrubbing everything in sight. Some of the parents helped, and we even scrubbed and calcimined the walls and ceiling.

It was time for a celebration, and Mama got busy with plans for a dance to raise money for books and supplies. During our confinement we had read every book of fiction in the school library. At Billy's insistence we even took turns reading *Alice Of Old Vincennes* aloud to each other. That's how desperate we were for reading material. It was as thick as a man's thigh, with tiny print, and dry as dust. We played countless games of hangman and tic-tac-toe on the blackboard and memorized long poems. My poem was *Lasca*, and I remember it word for word. The whole thing took nearly fifteen minutes to recite and started like this:

I sigh for the canter after the cattle
The crack of the whips like shots in battle
The melee of horns and hoofs and heads,
That wars and wrangles and scatters and spreads.

The poem ended with *Lasca* being killed in a cattle stampede, and it was enough to break your heart.

Everyone was ready for a break when Mama started planning the dance, and I looked forward to the new books Mama would buy with the proceeds from the midnight lunch even more than I did to the dance. One of the best times was when a big box of books came in the mail. I remember the satiny feel of the covers, the smell of new paper and ink, and the anticipation of all those as-yet-unread pages to savor.

We made posters of brightly colored construction paper advertising the dance. Mama made arrangements for a trip to Shawmut, and we distributed the posters. We brought home three-dozen loaves of "boughten" bread, a huge jar of dill pickles, and, best of all, an enormous jar of mayonnaise and pickle sandwich spread. We could hardly wait to taste the sandwiches. We all worked at making them and were allowed to have one for ourselves when they were finished.

It had been a long miserable time for us in quarantine, and we were ready for some fun. We especially looked forward to the music. People always brought their fiddles and accordions to these affairs, and there was usually someone who could play the school piano, even though it was badly out of tune. It seemed as though the drab old school buildings took on a magical transformation at Mama's dances and card parties. Maybe it was because everyone brought a lantern from home, and they were all lit and hanging from the rafters, or perhaps it was because everything was clean and scrubbed. Maybe it was because everyone wanted it to be special, and so it was.

I remember in particular one beautiful girl about my age who came from town with her parents for the program. She had brown eyes and long natural curls that bounced when she shook her head. She was aware of her beauty, and I burned with jealousy. She flirted shamelessly with Billy, and he lapped it up. "Some boys I abhor," she drawled, shaking her curls, "and some I adore." Billy blushed, and I made a face at him and went to watch the musicians tune their instruments and get ready to start.

I had skipped supper and was getting a headache. It was going to be a long time before we could eat, and the sandwiches were my favorite. I was so hungry that I couldn't wait, so I snitched a sandwich and hid in the cloakroom to eat it. After the first wonderful bite, the schoolhouse seemed to be spinning around me, and I sat down on the floor. I don't remember anything after that.

The next I knew I was in a terrible place with freezing winds and fiery forests, and the noises seemed to be piercing my eardrums. Devils and wild animals and flames surrounded me, and I could hear growling and moaning. I thought I must be in Hell, as little by little I began to wake up. Donna was beside me moaning and tossing, and Maribelle was standing over a stove, stirring something. When she saw that I was conscious she started to cry. Later when Donna awoke, she told us that we had been there for four days. We had been spirited out and taken to town where she could care for us, and we had been delirious all that time. The school board had found a little house where we could be moved. They were afraid the school would be closed for the rest of the term if word got out that there was another case of scarlet fever. Donna and I were very sick, but none of the other kids got it, and school went on as usual.

Poor Maribelle. What a responsibility for a young girl. Mama wasn't surprised when she announced that she wanted to be a nurse when she finished school. And when Maribelle took her nurse's exams she received the highest grade ever recorded in the state of Montana up until that time.

Moccasins

Mama could tell stories and make them seem so real that over the years we felt as though we had been there when it all happened. Her stories were even better than the books she read to us. Our favorite was the one about the time she had a dinner party she hadn't planned for.

My parents were living in the one-room homestead shack then, with just enough space for the big Monarch range, a table and two chairs, Mama's brass bed, and the oak rocking chair. After the hail came, Papa found a job with a threshing crew that would take him away until after Thanksgiving.

Mama was expecting their first child, and she was terrified at the thought of being alone, but she never admitted it to Papa. They would butcher the pig before he left, and she would have the lard to render, the jars of pork to can, and the bacon and ham to cure. She would be far too busy to be afraid, with the cow to milk and the chickens to care for, and she knew in her heart that her unreasonable fears about Indians were only left over from the stories her adoptive parents had told her.

Old Sam was the nearest neighbor, five miles to the west, and he was Will's friend, but the stories he liked to tell about the early days gave Mama the chills sometimes. The night before Papa and Sam left with the threshing crew he had told his favorite story again about the homesteader who had been staked over his own campfire. This time it was more than she could bear, and she burst into tears in spite of herself. Papa was angry, and she'd had a hard time convincing him that she could handle things by herself. Old Sam had been apologetic and tried to make amends.

"Why you ain't got no call to be askeered, Deely," he'd said. "They's good Indians and bad ones just like everybody else. I mind the time I'da been a goner if it hadn't been for old Mary. I was all rolled up in my blanket when I looked up and saw her a settin' on her horse quiet as a spook. 'Don't move . . . rattler,' she said. Well, she clumb down and poked up the fire and I didn't know who would get roasted out first, but we waited and that snake uncoiled and slid away into the sagebrush. If she'd have been some younger I'da kissed her. I tell you, I was sweatin', and it weren't from the fire."

The next morning Mama watched Papa and Sam drive away with the team and wagon and waved the dishtowel one last time as they disappeared over the hill.

"Were you scared, Mama?" we asked. "Did you worry about being alone?"

"Not then," she told us. The time went fast, and the days didn't seem long enough. The pork was all canned and sitting in pink rows on the shelves in the dugout cellar. The hams and bacon hung from the rafters down there, and she rubbed them with salt and brown sugar every other day. She had nearly finished the baby clothes and embroidered blue forget-me-nots on the new set of dishtowels when she heard the sound of horses. She thought it might be Mrs. Johnson, the woman who was coming to help her when her time came, and she whipped off her apron and patted her hair into place. When she flung the door open, she froze. There sat two young Indians on their ponies. They stared impassively at her while she stood there unable to make a move. Then they wheeled their ponies around the barn, scattering the squawking chickens, and raced on past the fence toward the buttes in the east.

"And then what happened, Mama?" we would always ask, although we knew the whole story by heart, and she would tell us how she took the rifle down and nearly used up all the shells as she tried to hit a baking powder can on the fence post.

The coyotes seemed to howl louder after that, or maybe it was that she wasn't sleeping as soundly. She crossed off each day on the calendar. It was 1914, and her due date, November 25, was heavily circled in red crayon. All the baby clothes were finished now and folded away in the basket under the bed. Will would be home soon, and the day before he was supposed to arrive she brought a slab of bacon up from the cellar and mixed up a batch of bread. She put a pot of beans in the oven and used the last of her dried apples for a pie. Will always said she made the best piecrust he had ever tasted.

When the floor was scrubbed and the windows gleaming, she sat down in the rocking chair. The afternoon sun stroked her cheek, and she fell deeply asleep. Something brushed her shoulder, and she jerked awake. An ancient Indian woman stood beside her, and Mama could see that the door was open and several young men were just outside, among them the two who had frightened her earlier. The old woman motioned them in. "I am Mary," she said, as though that explained everything. She pointed to the fresh loaves. "We are hungry."

One of the young men spied the rifle hanging on the wall. He took it down and ran his hands caressingly over the gleaming stock. The old woman spoke sharply, and he reluctantly put it back.

Mama said she used a whole pail of eggs and nearly the entire side of bacon before they had enough, but then one of the younger boys reached for Mama's pie, and that was the last straw. She tried to grab it out of his hands. "No! You may not have my husband's pie!"

The old woman laughed and motioned for the boy to put the pie back on the table. One of the young girls had opened the oven door and discovered the baking beans. She scooped a spoonful into her mouth, then dropped the spoon and spit the beans on the floor, clapping her hands to her burned mouth. The young men laughed, and Mary made a chopping motion with her hand. "Go now," she said, and then took the bacon and bread that was left and tied them in the dishtowel. Mama begged her to leave the bread, but she just shrugged. "You make more bread, got more meat," she said, then turned and placed both hands on Mama's bulging stomach. "Little one come when first snow flies," she said. Then, signaling the others, she mounted her horse and they rode away, never looking back. When Papa and Sam drove in that night they were disappointed to find a meager supper waiting for them.

There was a lot to be done to prepare for winter, and with Mama's advanced pregnancy she couldn't be as much help as she would have liked. Papa decided one morning to go and get Sam to help repair the roof on the chicken coop before winter set in. A chilly wind was blowing in from the north when he came galloping into the yard where Mama was feeding the chickens. "We've got trouble, Delia," he said. "Sam's horse stepped in a badger hole and threw him, and his leg is broken. Get your coat. We'll have to take him to the doctor."

"You don't need me," Mama told him. "I'll be all right, and besides, someone has to be here to take care of the animals in case you don't get home in time." Papa was doubtful about leaving her alone, but said he would be back as soon as he could, and this time he would be bringing Mrs. Johnson. "Just stay in the house until I get back. I'll do the chores when I get home," he said as he drove away.

Within an hour a light snow started to fall and the wind increased. Mama put on her coat and tied a scarf around her head. By the time she had milked and fed the cow and gathered the eggs the wind was at gale force, wrapping her long skirt around her legs and bending her almost double as she fought her way to the house. She lit the lamps and banked the fire and wondered if Papa would be home before morning.

She waited until ten o'clock and then went to bed, sure that she wouldn't be able to fall asleep, but she woke with a start to find that the wind had gone down and it was no longer snowing. It was two o'clock in the morning and she felt strange. When she got up to add coal to the fire, she discovered that the sheets were wet. It was then that the first pain crept across her back and clenched her stomach. But the baby wasn't due for three more weeks, and she wasn't prepared, she thought. What was she supposed to do? Boil water—yes, that's what they always did in the stories. She filled the kettle and put it on the back of the stove, and then the pains started coming closer together and harder. She removed the soiled sheets and re-made the bed and then collapsed in the rocking chair, moaning now with terror and pain. She heard the door open.

"Will?" she called. "Will?" A blanket-wrapped figure was bending over her. It was the old Indian woman, Mary, moving quickly into the room, making coffee and holding the cup for her to drink, massaging her stomach and her back, and then helping her into a squatting position.

"Baby come better this way. You push . . . push!" And she did push. Through a red haze of pain she heard the newborn cry, and then the guttural voice. "Fine baby. Big baby. You sleep. Sleep now," and she slept in spite of herself. When she awoke, Will and Mrs. Johnson were bending over her. Will was wearing a proud smile and cradling the baby in his arms. They told her Sam was in the hospital but would walk again, and Mary had left right after they arrived.

"She left this for you, though," Mrs. Johnson said, and handed Mama a rolled up dishtowel with blue flowers embroidered in the corner. When she opened the bundle, a small pair of beaded moccasins rolled out on the blanket.

"And what happened to the moccasins?" We always asked, and then she would bring them out and show them to us. "You all wore them when you were babies," she said, "and they never wore out. Maybe your children will wear them some day."

Cloudy Summer

It was May 1926, and school had been over for a week. Normally we would have been on our way to a summer job, but Mama was sick. Her bronchitis had flared up again, and it was worse than usual. She had written to her sister Myrtle in Great Falls for help and had grudgingly been told that there was a job as housekeeper for one of Myrtle's friends if she could get there in a week. Maribelle stayed in Big Sandy that summer, working at the Big Store.

"We'll meet the train," my aunt had said, "and you and the kids can come to us for a few days until you can find a place."

Mr. Valsted said he would take us to the train station as soon as we were ready, and although Mama was too weak to help with the packing, we knew the drill. With Billy in charge, we set to work.

First we emptied the washstand and cupboard, both made from orange crates, and took down the cretonne curtains that covered our makeshift clothes closet. We packed the crates with dishes and cooking utensils, Mama's "left-handed" hammer, the curtains and towels. Next came the part we liked the best. We dragged the homemade ticking mattresses out and dumped their contents into a pile for burning. We had filled them with new straw in the fall and brought them in smelling of sunshine and clean Montana air. Now they smelled of stale sweat and winter. We folded the blankets and pillows into the mattresses and rolled them up, securing them with the clothesline rope. We traveled light, so anything that wasn't absolutely necessary was jettisoned and thrown into the burn pile in the yard, along with the straw that had filled the ticking.

The three items that made the one-room teacherages home were Mama's brass bedstead, her sewing machine, and the old oak rocking chair, the only things she had brought to her marriage. We ticketed these for shipping, and the job was almost done. Smoke from the bonfire rose against the brilliant blue sky as Mr. Valsted's truck came rattling down the road.

Mama was still weak, and the schoolhouse looked forlorn and empty, but the birds were building their nests, and the meadowlarks were singing their insistent tune. Even today I cannot hear a meadowlark without thinking of Mama. Whenever we worried, she pointed them out, saying, "Listen to the meadowlarks, children. Everything will be alright."

To the trill of meadowlarks we once more bid goodbye to our surroundings and headed toward an uncertain future. The train was already in the station when we pulled up. It didn't take long to unload our few possessions from the truck and check the big items. Mama motioned Billy aside. "Take this money," she said, "and buy one whole fare and two half fares while I get the little girls settled."

"But," Billy whispered, "how about the kids?"

"Just get the tickets," she said, "and pray."

"Well, Mrs. Hanson," Mr. Valsted said, shaking her hand, "I hate to see you go. If it had been up to me, you coulda stayed forever, but times is hard. With the extra fuel to heat the schoolhouse at night—well, you know how it is."

Mama gave him a watery smile. "I certainly do. I'll surely miss those children, though."

"You did a lot for us." Mr. Valsted reached for his handkerchief and dabbed at his eyes. "You know, Blackie wants to go to high school now, and his mother sticks up for him. She's even talking about college now. Of course, if he don't change his ways, the state reform school in Miles City is the only college he'll be going to."

"You underestimate that young man," Mama said, "He'll make you proud someday."

Mr. Valsted gave her a long look, thumped Billy on the back, hugged the little girls, and headed for the truck, pocketing his handkerchief.

We were all a little teary, and Irene, Donna, and Betty Lou were whining as we boarded the train. They wanted to sit up and look out the window, but Mama made them lie down on the seats and we covered them up with their coats. Irene was still protesting when Billy and I took our seats.

Mama's face had changed from pasty white to a deep flush, and she was hot when I touched her hand. The train gave a shuddering moan, and we were moving down the tracks. The conductor was heading our way, taking tickets and exchanging pleasantries with the passengers. Billy and I looked at each other, crossing our fingers when he stopped at our seats. Mama turned her head to the window and handed him the tickets. He fanned them out. "Three tickets here, that right?"

Mama just looked at him and blushed an even deeper red. She nodded and turned her head to the window again. He stood there for what was probably about a minute but it seemed much longer. Reaching down, he lifted a corner of one of the coats. Bette scowled, and Donna flashed her dimples as tears rolled out of her big blue eyes. Irene was sulking. They looked at each other and then he dropped the coat. "My, my, three little ones all under the age of six." He ruffled Billy's hair. "Take care of your Mama, son. Ma'am, you don't look too good, if you don't mind my saying so. Better get some rest before we pull into the Falls. Looks like you'll need it."

I thought I heard Mama say, "God bless that man," as he walked away.

She was soon asleep in spite of herself, although she tried to stay awake. Her breathing sounded raspy and hoarse, and she seemed to be moaning in her sleep, "cold . . . I'm so cold." I touched her face, and she was very hot. Saying, "watch the kids," Billy hurried down the aisle and disappeared. When he came back, he had the conductor with him. The conductor felt Mama's forehead. "Your mother is pretty sick, son," he said. "Will someone be there to meet you when you get in?"

"I think . . . my Aunt Myrtle."

He scribbled on a piece of paper and gave it to Billy. "This isn't the end of my run," he said, "so I can't help much, but if you need a place to stay, give this to the clerk at the hotel across the street from the station. Good luck, kid."

The cinders flew and the train belched smoke as we pulled into Great Falls. It was already dark, but Mama didn't seem to notice as we bundled her into her coat. She felt almost boneless, as though the starch that had held her together all these years had just drained away.

I was glad for once that Billy was giving orders. We needed help, and Mama needed it most of all. Somehow we got them all into the station. I ran back and forth, peering into each face, saying, "Aunt Myrtle?" but no one even looked my way. Finally, when the station was empty, and we knew our aunt wasn't coming, we left, leading Mama along with the kids, and headed for the hotel.

Mama was delirious, and she staggered, not seeming to know where she was. We must have been a sorry sight when we walked up to the desk. Billy handed the clerk the message, and he rang for the bellboy as he handed a key to Mama. She held it in her hand and made no move to go. "Well, you got a room," he said, "What ya waitin' for? You're drunk, lady, and if I had my way, you wouldn't be stayin' here!"

"She's sick." Billy was enraged.

"Okay," the clerk said, "take 'em up to Tom's room and give 'em some extra blankets. They must be some more of Tom's strays. He'll be on the street himself one of these days if he don't watch out."

Thank God for the "Toms" of this world.

For two days, Mama slipped in and out of delirium. The manager came up to see how we were getting along, and then told us to go to Eddie's Bakery and ask for yesterday's baking. When we found the place, two scruffy young men were leaning against the building smoking, and one of them said, "lookin' for handouts, kids?"

I was angry and humiliated when they told us to go around to the back door and wait. We waited for at least twenty minutes and when they showed up at last, they looked at each other and laughed as they handed us the sack. I've never been able to eat butterhorns since.

When we returned with the bread, Mama gave Billy a dime and told him to get a package of bouillon cubes. I'm not sure if that was her last dime or not, but it must have been pretty close. We dissolved them in hot water from the sink and got her to drink several cups of it. She couldn't swallow any bread, but she seemed to gain a little of her strength back. Aunt Myrtle and Uncle Charlie eventually tracked us down, and both Mama and Aunt Myrtle blamed the other for the mix-up. Not a very good beginning for a visit with our relatives.

Mama rented a tiny basement apartment, and we pretty much looked after ourselves. We chased the iceman for chips of sparkling ice on hot days and played run-sheep-run in the long evenings with the neighborhood kids. The job as housekeeper was no longer open, but pale and weak as she was, Mama found a position as assistant pastry cook and soon built such a reputation for her succulent pies that people from all over town came to sample them.

Uncle Charlie was one of those loud-talking fellows with plans for making it big. His current project was raising a hundred chickens on his half-acre place, three miles out in the country, and planting the rest in corn. He didn't like hoeing or tending chickens very much, so he gave the job to Billy and me. He had curly blond hair and beguiling blue eyes, and you couldn't believe a word he said. He had visions of platters of fried chicken and tubs of fresh corn on the cob that he would sell at the state fair and make "a bundle." Uncle Charlie's fondness for the horses kept him flat broke, but he always knew that a big score was just around the corner. He promised to pay us five dollars a week, but somehow the money was never available when it was time to pay up.

Poor Aunt Myrtle. She was a dumpy bottle blond, and she imagined that there was a floozy waiting around every corner to entrap her Charlie. I think she even suspected Mama. He didn't make things any easier, either, by being extra courtly around Mama. They had two beautiful children, a boy, age eight, and a girl, age six, and they were Aunt Myrtle's reason for living. She was always stuffing them with cake and other goodies, and they were already showing signs of obesity. Their father largely ignored them except for an occasional absent-minded pat on the head.

As it turned out, we didn't stay in Great Falls very long. Mama came home one night looking worse than ever. She had a hoarse cough and was running a temperature. The next morning she couldn't go to work. When she was able to go back, they told her the job was filled. "You were using too much shortening in the pies anyway," they said.

Our Friend Horst

It was panic time. The rent was due and with Mama still so sick we had to depend on Aunt Myrtle again. She took care of the little girls along with her own two while Billy and I were out hoeing, anyway. When Mama received a letter with a contract from a school in the mountains out of Big Sandy we all cheered, but we still had to have a place to go for the rest of the summer and a way to get there. Since Aunt Myrtle had been planning a trip back east, it was decided that she would take the little girls back to the aunts in Minnesota.

Just when our predicament seemed insurmountable, we received a letter from our old friend Horst. He had sent away for a mail order bride within a year of when we left, and he was happy as a barnyard rooster. He had heard of our troubles and wanted to help. His bride, he said, would nurse Mama back to health. He knew of a family who would take me for the summer, and Billy wouldn't have any trouble finding a place to work.

He himself would make the long drive to Great Falls and take us home with him. "My Olga," he wrote us, "She can outwork any man, and she can cook almost as good as you, Mrs. Lady." Then poking her slyly, he wrote, "I could have got a better one if I'd had more time."

It was a long tiring trip from Great Falls to the Glasgow area, and Mama was worn out. When we drove into the yard we were greeted by Olga, who was the embodiment of a Viking woman, with thick flaxen hair that hung in a braid to her ample waist. Her bright blue eyes sparkled when she caught sight of her "little fella," and she swooped him up in her arms and planted large wet kisses on both cheeks. He watched with pride as she embraced us all. "We will get you well," she told Mama. "Lots of good eggs und butter und cream. I nurse plenty women in old country. You rest und eat now."

I wept when I had to say goodbye to my brother. He was going to work for a pair of bachelor brothers, and it seemed then that our family would never be the same again. I started to sniffle again when we saw another car coming down the road. Olga knelt and looked into my eyes. "These are good kind people, and you must be good girl while your Mama get well. Dat poor little Missus, she want little girl like you, but doctor say not possible."

I wasn't going to make it easy and hid behind the sofa when the Ransoms came to get me. He was a tidy, good-looking man with a trim moustache, and was wearing a dress-up suit, not at all like the men I had been used to seeing. She was a tiny little woman, with eyes like blue pansies, and curly black hair that I would have given anything for, but I didn't care if she was pretty. I wasn't going to like her. Their son, Harold, had been staring at me with his pop-eyes, and when we shook hands all round he squeezed my hand until my eyes watered. I knew right then that we would never be friends.

They told me all about the pretty little town of Saco and said they were sure I would find friends quickly. "You'll have your own room, won't that be nice?" Mrs. Ransom said. At that I burst into tears and cried all the louder. I was used to cuddling with my sisters, and the idea of sleeping alone made me even more reluctant to go. Mama was crying too by this time, but she said I would have to be a big girl and go with them. When they told me that I would have a horse to ride every day, I allowed myself to be convinced. Amid hiccups and awash with tears, I watched out the window of the car as we drove down the road, and Horst's stark farmhouse disappeared in a cloud of dust.

It seemed like forever before we drove through the little town of Saco, and when Mr. Ransom passed the barbershop, he said, "This is mine, and now we'll show you where you will be going to school this fall." I saw Mrs. Ransom poke him, and I felt as though I had just swallowed an icicle. Go to school here? That wasn't part of the bargain. I was going to school with my mother, just as I always had.

When we turned in at the gate, I could see that the Ransoms' home was nicer than any place I had ever lived. There were lilac trees in bloom and a small flower garden in the yard, surrounded by green grass. Mrs. Ransom took me by the hand, her eyes shining with pride. "Let me show you to your room. You're going to love it," she said.

It was pretty, with white lace curtains and a pink bedspread, but I wasn't going to admit it to her. If I had just known—she was the only person in that household who was on my side. I unpacked my few clothes in the room that was to be all my own and thought over the events of the past week. I had been separated from my brother and sisters and had watched as Mama grew weaker and more drawn and worried. I promised then, making one of my many bargains with God, that I would do as I was told and be a good girl, if He would just make Mama well so we could all be together again.

That night after the supper dishes were done, Mrs. Ransom stayed with me in the bathroom, and I didn't like it. Even in the small quarters we were used to, we hung a blanket over a wire for privacy at bath time. "I always wanted a little girl of my own," she said, "and I thought this was what mothers do."

"I'm eight years old," I told her, "and I don't need any help with my bath, Mrs. Ransom."

She flinched and then pulled my chin up and looked at me. "I was hoping you would call me Mother." There were tears in her eyes.

Oh boy, this one is going to be easy, I thought. It would be hard to keep my promise to be a good little girl when she was such a pushover. When she came to hear my prayers and tuck me in I just murmured, "Goodnight," and turned my face to the wall.

The next day I was introduced to Bud, the horse. They showed me how to get the bit in his mouth and how to bridle him, and even how to climb up on the manger and put his saddle on. Mostly I rode him bareback, and I loved the freedom of galloping through the pasture with my hair blowing in the wind. I never got tired of it and sometimes felt that he was my only friend. For a few days things went pretty smoothly, but I hadn't reckoned on Harold.

He was a spoiled brat who resented my presence and never lost an opportunity to make my life miserable. I kept out of his way as much as possible for the first few weeks, but when I least expected it, he would pounce and twist my arms or pull my hair. When I threatened to tell his mother, he said, "Think anyone's going to believe you, orphan? Nobody likes you, and my mother can hardly wait to send you back." This was exactly what I wanted to hear, and my hopes rose for an early reunion with my family, but nobody said anything about sending me home.

I made it a point to hang around corners and listen when Mrs. Ransom had company, and one day I heard my name mentioned. "Aren't you a little worried about having that child here when her mother has T.B.?" It was the nearest neighbor, the one with the skinny legs and pinched nose. I sat perfectly still under the table. She always had some juicy gossip, although Mrs. Ransom never encouraged her. This time a trickle of fear ran down my back.

"She doesn't have T.B.," Mrs. Ransom said. "She has chronic bronchitis that sometimes turns into pneumonia."

"Well, that's not the way I heard it," Nosey said.

I listened hard as the visitor leaned over and whispered, "Have you signed the papers for adoption yet?"

Adoption?! I crept closer. Mrs. Ransom sounded troubled.

"No, we've decided to wait and see if she gets along in school. And then there's Harold. He resents her so, and I know he has been mean to her, although she has never tattled. And she has been so good, just the little girl I always wanted. She does her chores without complaining and is reasonably good-natured, although—there is something else. She doesn't seem to warm up to me at all."

"That will change, once she realizes she's a real part of your family," the neighbor said. "She's not a very pretty little thing, though. Maybe you should wait."

I heard Mrs. Ransom gasp. "She's pretty to me," she said, "and I think that was an awful thing to say!" At that moment I came close to liking that woman.

What should I do? I wondered. I didn't want to be a part of this family, ever. I had been doing it all wrong. I wasn't going to be a "good little girl" anymore. Things would be different from now on.

The next morning I didn't get up when I was called and complained of a headache when it was time to do the dishes. Although I had been cautioned never to take the horse out unless I told someone first, I slipped out and was soon flying through the pasture. Then, after riding him until he was in a sweat, I tied him up in the barn without feeding and watering him first, and didn't take his bridle off.

When Harold came running in all bright-eyed, with his father behind him, I knew I was in for it. "Did you take Bud out without asking?" Mr. Ransom said. I looked at the floor and nodded my head. "Did you leave him in the barn without food and water?" Again I nodded. "Well then, it looks like you'll be losing your riding privileges for a week. Do you have anything to say for yourself?"

I still just hung my head. "No," I whispered.

"Maybe you should go to your room and stay there until you can think of a reason for mistreating poor old Bud," he said.

Harold looked at me triumphantly, and I stuck out my tongue at him as I turned and left the room.

"I can't imagine what has gotten into her. She's been so good and obedient up until now," Mrs. Ransom said. "Don't you think you're being a little harsh, taking away her riding privileges for a whole week?"

He shook his head. "No. I don't know what her reason was, but it's clear that she did this deliberately."

I planned the next move in my crusade to be as obnoxious as possible. I left half of the dusting undone, spilled my milk at the supper table, and broke dishes just often enough that I was relieved of the dish wiping detail. But it was almost time for school to start, and I was getting no closer to my goal of being sent back to Mama.

"We're going to do something really exciting, dear," Mrs. Ransom said one day. "How would you like to go to Great Falls and shop for school clothes?" Then, before I could tell her that I thought the clothes I had were good enough, she said we'd go out for dinner and a movie afterwards. I was hooked. I had never been to a movie. The closest was when Mama came home from teacher's convention and told us in detail about the one she had seen, singing the songs, and making the story come alive for us.

I don't remember the shopping, but I remember that movie. When we entered the theater and smelled the popcorn, my head swam with sensations. The name of the movie was *The Hunchback of Notre Dame*, starring Lon Chaney, and the piano player on the stage played thundering music while we read the dialogue on the screen. I would just get immersed in the story, and then I would think about my family, and about how much better it would have been seeing it with them. Somehow seeing the movie without them wasn't as thrilling as I had thought it would be. Listening to Mama tell about it was better.

When school began I could imagine the first day of school the way it had always been with Mama, and my spirits sank lower than ever. I had been so sure that I would be back with my family by then. We walked the mile to town, joined by three other children from the next farm, so Harold couldn't be quite as mean as usual. A railroad track ran parallel to the road, and I wondered how it would be, walking over the trestle, and shivered at the thought of meeting a train on the way across.

I had a brand new red lunch box, and it was filled, I knew, with goodies. The first thing I did when I got to school was hide it. When lunchtime came around, I sat forlornly in my seat while the other kids opened their lunches and ate. My mouth watered, but I wasn't going to give in. When the teacher noticed that I wasn't eating, she asked me about it. "I don't have a lunch," I told her. When the Ransoms heard about this, they would surely send me home, I thought. On the way home I lagged behind the others and greedily ate the lunch that had been so lovingly prepared for me.

Within a week I met a girl who was the child of a friend of Mrs. Ransom. She always walked home at noon to have lunch with her mother, and I thought this was a wonderful way to live, having lunch with your mother every day. When I told her that I didn't have any lunch, she asked me to come with her. This was almost the last straw. When the Ransoms found out about my deceitfulness, they asked me again why I had done such a thing. When I just shrugged my shoulders, they looked baffled.

They still didn't say anything about sending me back to Mama after all my meanness, and I was about ready to give up. One day Mrs. Ransom pulled me onto her lap despite my struggles. "You and I need to have a talk," she said. My chest felt like it had a balloon in it that was just about to burst. I was going to be adopted, and there wasn't anything I could do about it.

"I know you are aware that we have been trying to talk your mother into letting us adopt you. I saw you under the table that day when I was discussing it with my neighbor." It seemed that all the blood in my body rushed to my head, and I felt as though I were going to faint. My ears were ringing and I could barely hear what she was saying. "Listen to me," she said, as I continued to try to pull away from her. "Since then you have changed from a lovely little girl into a spiteful and deceitful little harridan. You behave as though you hate me. Have I done anything to cause you to feel this way?"

I gulped, and then the words poured out as I told her of my fear of leaving my family, of how I worried that Mama would get sick again and I wouldn't be there to help her, of how much I missed my brother and little sisters, and, finally, about being afraid of Harold.

"I know Harold has been tormenting you, dear," she said. "I'm keeping an eye on him, but I don't think he'll do anything really bad. It's just normal jealousy, I think. After all, he's been the only child around here for twelve years."

"Here," she said, "I want to show you this. It came just yesterday." She handed me a letter, and I recognized Mama's distinctive writing. In it Mama said I could come home as soon as she got her first paycheck and could send me the train fare. I was so happy I hugged Mrs. Ransom and promised her that I would change back into the good girl I had been.

As it turned out I wouldn't have had to do anything to be sent back to Mama. Harold did it for me. I had relaxed my watchfulness, and one day after a ride, when I was currying old Bud, Harold grabbed me and pushed me against the hay bales, holding my hands above my head. I automatically came up with my knee and gave him such a jolt to the chin that he bit his tongue clear through. He ran for the house, screaming with pain, with blood dripping down his chin. Mr. Ransom loaded him into the car and said, "I've had enough! Have her clothes packed when I get home."

That afternoon a telegram was sent to my mother, and I was on the train the next morning. How different that train trip was from the one we all took in the spring. I was on my way to Big Sandy and from there to another adventure in the Bear's Paw Mountains. Mrs. Ransom was crying when the train arrived at the Saco station. Harold couldn't say anything with his injured tongue, but the look he gave me contained the venom of a thousand vipers. I didn't care. My mind was already at the station in Big Sandy where my family would be waiting for me, and I was happy at last.

Mountain School

I was giddy with happiness and felt as though I had just been let out of jail when the train pulled out of Saco and headed for Big Sandy. I would be back with my family in time for Thanksgiving, and I had a lot to be thankful for. It was a heady feeling, riding the train by myself. I felt all grown up and ready for new adventures, and I could hardly wait. When the train whistled I knew we were getting close, and I pressed my face against the window, straining to see them. Yes, there they were. When I got off the train I threw myself at Mama and burst into tears, hugging her fiercely. "Don't cry now," she said. "We're together again and everything will be fine," but I couldn't stop. It seemed that all the tears I had held inside during that lonely summer had to be cried out.

The first thing I noticed when I stopped crying was that Mama looked different. She had lost a lot of weight and wasn't as cuddly as she had been. She still looked pale and tired, but her smile was as bright and welcoming as always. Billy crossed his eyes at me and punched my arm, his usual gesture of affection. I was awfully glad to see him, I can tell you, after having had to dodge horrible Harold.

"This is our driver, Mr. Carlson," Mama said. He was a pleasant looking man, but he appeared worried.

"We had better get on the road," he said. "This storm could get nasty." The truck had seen better days and had a broken window on the driver's side that wouldn't close. Snow was drifting in, making it hard for him to see. Billy and I climbed in the back and we had to hang on to keep from being bounced from one side to the other.

There had been a light snow falling when they met me at the train station, and it was turning into a real snowstorm. We were barely out of town when the old truck began to slip and slide around the curves. We almost didn't make it over the first hill.

"The roads could be blocked by the time we get there if she keeps on like this," Mr. Carlson said. "You all might have to get out and walk up the next hill. Think you can make it, Mrs. Hanson?"

Of course we could make it, but we weren't too sure about the truck. The snow was thick and wet and clingy. I hadn't buckled my overshoes—fashion dictated wearing them unbuckled—and they were filled with snow when we reached the top. The old truck shimmied and shook halfway up the hill and then backed down for another run at it. Mr. Carlson almost made it, but he had to try it again before the truck finally chugged over the hill. We still had seven miles of snowy road ahead of us, but we were finally on our way, and I could hardly wait to see my sisters.

Two of the families were waiting, laden with blankets and provisions, when we arrived at the schoolhouse. The custom was that the children would stay with the teacher when the roads were blocked, and it was happening earlier than anyone had planned for. The noise and general hubbub made me feel as though I was home at last. I was so glad to see my sisters. Irene and Donna and I jumped up and down, hugging each other, but they told me that Bette had developed a kidney infection and had had to stay with the aunts in Minneapolis.

While everyone else was busy getting settled, I looked the place over. The schoolhouse had just been built that year, and it smelled of new wood and floor wax and fresh varnish. It was a much larger building than the old schoolhouse had been, they said, with the teacher's quarters and two extra rooms as part of the main structure. We were surrounded by trees such as I had never seen before. There were great junipers with curving branches that swept to the ground, almost inviting you to make a hammock of them. All of this was set in a little valley. With fresh snow piling along the branches I felt as though we were inside one of those glass paper weights that you shake to make the snow swirl around the little house inside.

When two more sleds pulled up and spilled their load of children, it was easy to see why the two extra rooms had been built. In they came, bearing sacks of potatoes, beans, a slab of beef, and a ham. There were quart jars of home-canned vegetables and large sacks of flour and brown sugar and oatmeal. It was a bonanza, a wealth of provisions such as our family had never seen before.

One wagon was full of Hendersons. The father, Dick, had a toothpick in the corner of his mouth, which he shifted back and forth from time to time. He had an amused way of squinting his eyes when he talked that made him look as though he thought life was a huge joke, and he was the only one who knew the punch line. He had been married twice and was the father of a large family of six boys and four girls. The older boys had all left home as soon as they discovered that they didn't have to labor twelve hours a day when they worked for someone other than their father. The mother of the girls was a hugely fat woman who laughed a lot, and I liked her immediately. She wore a man's shirt over her dress and mismatched socks, and she looked exactly right.

One of the other fathers had a curly black beard and a bushy mustache. When he came in with his wife and daughter trailing behind, he lost no time in letting everyone know who was in charge. "I am Mathew Goodman, school board chairman," he said.

His wife stood timidly behind him, her head bent under the weight of a braided coronet of glistening brown hair. With her slender neck she reminded me of a flower that was too heavy for its stem. The daughter had hair that hung to her waist and rippled in the thin light. I thought she was the most beautiful girl I had ever seen.

"My Sara is here to study and learn, but she will read her Bible and her school books only," Mr. Goodman said. "She is to help with the chores and say her prayers daily. Her Mother and I gave her life so she could do God's work. Remember that, Sara."

"Yes, Papa," Sarah said, and she turned her head away, trying to hide the tears of embarrassment that threatened to roll down her cheeks.

"Those are the rules," Goodman said, and touched her shoulder lightly. Then, lifting a strand of her glorious hair, he let it slide slowly through his fingers.

The Henderson girls were Martha, Wilma, Freda, and Pearl, the oldest fourteen and the youngest eleven. They were all good-natured like their mother and turned out to be good cooks. The Carlsons had three big boys with already deepening voices, and they looked like trouble. The Davises were a tidy little couple who didn't have much to say. They were exactly the same size, with short graying hair. They even looked alike. They reminded me of a pair of salt and peppershakers. Bonnie was their only child, and taller than her parents, although she was only twelve. She had a little kewpie doll face that seemed incongruous with her muscular build, but her parents flushed with pride whenever they looked at her.

Mama made a pot of coffee and brought out a big box of store-bought doughnuts that disappeared like magic. The parents left soon after that and the rest of the day was spent getting everyone settled. Cots were set up and clothes put away, and the two bedrooms were crowded to bursting. My sisters and I slept in a bed set up in one corner of the schoolroom, but Billy bunked with the other boys. Nothing could have pleased him more after being surrounded by females all his life.

It was still snowing in the morning, but fixing breakfast for all those hungry kids was a snap for the big girls. They had done this before and had a routine all worked out. They took over the cooking and the rest of us girls took turns washing the dishes. The big boys chopped the wood and kept the fires going, and school went on as usual. The kids were used to boarding with the teacher. When the weather cleared enough the roads would be dug out, and they would go home again until the next big snow.

The roads were still blocked at Thanksgiving time, and although the snow was waist high in some places, the three Carlson boys and the Henderson girls decided to walk home for the weekend. The sun came out, touching the tops of the trees, turning our valley into a glory of blue and white and gold, and Mama sent the rest of us out to get some exercise and fresh air. Great clumps of snow came sliding down those swooping branches, burying much of the schoolyard. We all took turns shoveling out the paths to the boys' and girls' outhouses. We built a huge snowman and made snow angels until we were exhausted. It was a pleasure being mostly by ourselves again, and we celebrated the holiday with enthusiasm. Although we did enjoy having the other kids around, it was beginning to wear thin. But I had a lot to be thankful for, and I never forgot it for a minute.

With Thanksgiving behind us we began making plans for the Christmas program. Things were going along nicely when Sara came to Mama with a complaint. "My garters are missing, teacher, and I can't keep my stockings up." Mama gave her a length of elastic to make new garters, but the next morning Bonnie came with the news that her hair ribbons were gone. "And I think I know who took 'em," she said.

The girls had been getting along fairly well, but now they were scarcely speaking to each other. Mama threatened to discontinue reading at noon if their bickering didn't stop. Other small items were missing: a powder-puff, a barrette, and then some of the boy's belongings, a sock, a handkerchief. It was becoming almost impossible to concentrate on schoolwork, let alone our parts in the Christmas program.

It was obvious that the other girls, led by Bonnie, were giving Sara the cold shoulder. They had decided to blame her for all the missing articles because her father wouldn't allow her to wear any ornaments at home. They teased her about her long hair and the ankle-length, ugly dresses and heavy boots she had to wear. Actually it didn't make any difference what she wore, she was still the prettiest of all of them, I thought. When bath time came around Sara always complained that her hair was too long and thick, and she begged Mama to cut it for her. All of the other girls had the wind-blown bobs that were so stylish then, and she wanted to be like the rest.

"Sara, you know your father would be very angry," Mama said. "Just try to be patient. I'm sure he'll come around when he sees how much it means to you."

"You don't know him. He says it is evil, that only men can cut their hair. He says the Bible forbids it. He would never allow me!"

Mama patted her shoulder and gave her a little hug. "Run along now and study your part in the play."

The day before the program a strong wind blew in across the mountain that shook the trees and rattled the windows and melted most of the snowdrifts. There was excitement in the air, and the holiday feeling was upon us. Mama was making last minute alterations on some of the costumes and couldn't find her scissors. Everyone scattered, looking for them, but they were no place to be found. She looked thoughtful. "Has anyone seen Sara?" she asked. "Stay in your seats, all of you." She put on her coat and went outside. Of course we ran to the windows and watched as she opened the door to the girl's toilet.

A weeping Sara stepped out and handed Mama the scissors. Long strands of hair fell from her shoulders into the snow. Mama put her arms around the girl and led her inside, telling the rest of us to just go along with our studies.

"Papa will be so angry," Sara wailed. "He'll never forgive me. Never."

"Maybe he won't feel so angry when I get it trimmed up for you," Mama told her.

"Oh, would you please?" Sara continued to cry as Mama wielded the scissors. I thought she looked as pretty as ever with her short bouncing curls, but the older girls snickered.

"There'll be no more of that," Mama ordered. "Now get to work, all of you." After the tension of the day we relaxed as we decorated the schoolhouse and trimmed the tree. I think it was the prettiest tree I had ever seen. We popped a huge bowl of popcorn and decorated the tree with strings of popcorn and red and green paper chains. We hung boughs of juniper over the windows and doors, and when we sprinkled juniper needles on the stove it began to look and smell like Christmas.

The next morning there were howls of outrage from the girl's bedroom. Bonnie, red-faced and angry, was accusing Sara of taking her brand new ribbon that she had been saving for this special occasion. She claimed that she had put it out with the rest of her clothes the night before, and it was gone. The other girls thought they should be allowed to look through Sara's things, which Sara would not allow.

"I'll sort through everything here, and if we don't find it you'll just have to use your old one," Mama said. "We simply don't have the time to keep on looking."

Bonnie never missed a chance to belittle Sara. "Everyone knows that Sara's father won't let her wear any ribbons, so it has to be her."

"That will be enough!" Mama said.

"You boys get your coats on and fill the tubs with snow, and I want you girls to help make a batch of donuts."

"You're a liar and a thief," Bonnie whispered to Sara, "and I hope your old man lays into you good!"

Mama scowled at her. "I said we'll sort this out later. Now come on and help with the donuts!" Sara turned pale, but she worked right along with the others, tight lipped and saying nothing.

The snow was melting on the stoves, and the smell of fresh donuts filled the air. Mama helped the boys string the wire and hang the sheets that were to form a curtain for the stage. When the baths were over the girls mopped all the floors with the bath water. Since the kids were staying at school we had practiced the Christmas play until everyone knew each other's parts, so there wasn't any need for another rehearsal. Bonnie had the part of a ragged gypsy woman who came to beg from the beautiful lady of the cottage, played by Sara.

Mama took the two girls aside. "I hope you girls won't mind too much," she said, "but there are going to be some changes made. I'm sure this sounds difficult, but you know the play so well that I have no doubt you can handle it. Sara, I want you to change roles with Bonnie." Sara stared, her mouth quivering as Bonnie gave her a gloating look.

"I think this arrangement might be the best thing for both of you." She winked at Sara who nodded, a sudden look of understanding on her face, and the girls began to change clothes. When Mama draped the gold fringed piano scarf over Sara's short curls, and pinned it under her chin, it was plain to see why she had made the change. She knew there would be trouble later, but at least she could put it off until after the program.

Mathew Goodman and his wife were the first to arrive. "Where is my Sara?" he said.

"She's back helping the younger ones with their costumes," Mama told him. "But why don't you have a fresh donut and a glass of cider while I go and see if she can get away?"

"She will come now. It is not to see if she can get away." He handed his coat to his wife who scurried off to hang it up.

"I'll try, but here, have a donut," Mama said. "The girls worked very hard to get them ready for our guests tonight." Mathew snorted, then reached for a donut, and with a nod indicated that his wife could have one, too. Mama ladled out the cider and went back to the bedroom to talk to Sara, who was pale and shaking. "Now please try to relax," she told her. "Your father is here and wants to see you. Your mother, too, of course."

"I c-c-can't," Sara said, shaking her head.

"Alright then, come out and wave to them and I'll explain that you're busy. But Sara, you have to pull yourself together at least until after the program is over. I won't allow you to spoil the evening for the others."

Just then other wagonloads of parents began to arrive, and the donuts and hot cider were passed around. "We have a slight case of opening night nerves," Mama whispered to the Goodmans, "and I need Sara and the rest of the big girls right now. Everyone please take your seats and we'll get started." Sara stepped out from behind the curtains and waved at her parents, and this seemed to satisfy Mathew for the moment.

The play moved along smoothly, everyone remembering their parts, and as the students came out in turn to take a bow there was a commotion in the back of the room. Santa Claus came in, carrying a sack over his shoulder, followed by the Hendersons with a big box of apples to be shared. Mama gave a prayer of thanks that the storm she knew was brewing could be put off a little longer. Carols were sung, presents were distributed, and then it was time to take off the costumes and go home for two weeks of vacation.

The tension was almost thick enough to touch. It was as if we had all drawn a breath at the same time. Mathew Goodman held Sara's coat as she reluctantly came out of the bedroom with her box of things. Mathew froze. "What happened to your hair?" He grabbed her by the shoulders and shook her. "Sara, who cut your hair?"

She looked down at the floor. "Teacher did it," she said.

Mathew was livid. "You . . . YOU . . . dared to cut my daughter's hair?" he roared.

"Tell the truth, Sara," Mama said.

"Daughter, are you lying to me?" Everyone was watching and listening.

"No, Papa, I'm not lying. The teacher cut my hair."

"You see, my daughter does not lie. If she says you cut her hair then that is the way of it. We'll leave now, and Sara will go to school at home."

"Sara does lie!" It was Bonnie who spoke up. "Ask her where she hid all the things she took."

"Just a minute, now," Mama said. "I've been hearing about all the stolen articles, and I don't think it's fair to blame each other. Do any of you have an extra lantern?"

One of the Carlson boys brought one from their sleigh while the other two pushed Mama's desk under a trapdoor in the ceiling. One of the boys grabbed Billy and boosted him up through the little door, handing him the lantern, and after he had set the trapdoor aside we could hear him bumping around up there. He gave us a dusty grin as he pushed a shower of articles through the trap door. There it all was, the ribbons, a powder puff, garters, all woven into a delicate little nest.

Packrats!

An audible sigh passed around the room. Mathew looked stunned.

"Don't you think you girls owe Sara an apology for accusing her of being a thief?" Mama said. They all hung their heads and mumbled. Finally, first one and then another of the girls went up and put their arms around Sara.

Mathew Goodman shouted above the noise. "First, you say my Sara is a liar, and now you call her a thief! Mrs. Hanson cuts my daughter's hair without my permission. What kind of an example is she setting for the children? I say we call a meeting and give her notice."

Sara broke away from the circle of girls and faced her father. "Papa, I cut my own hair."

Mathew stared at her, his face turning white and then fiery red, and he seemed to wilt. "You lied to your father?" he said incredulously.

"No Papa, I didn't really lie, because she did cut it, but it was only to even it up after I had made it look so awful. It was just that I didn't tell all of the truth." She turned to Mama. "I'm so sorry and ashamed. Can you ever forgive me? Please, please forgive me."

Mathew continued to glare at the girl as his wife took a determined step forward. "You are a good daughter," she said, drawing her toward the door. "Get your coat, Mathew. We'll come by tomorrow on our way to town and help you clean up, Mrs. Hanson, and then we're going to talk this over. Mathew, your coat!"

He looked at her in wonderment, as though she were suddenly speaking a foreign language. "All right, Esther," he said.

The Candy Bar

Consider how it must have been for our mother, cooped up all day with other people's children and then in the long winter evenings with the five of us. She managed by doing what she did best: she read to us, and how she read. We roamed the caves with Huck and Becky and Tom. We were Riders of the Purple Sage. We were Anthony and Cleopatra and Paris and Helen of Troy. She read to us by the light of the setting sun. She read to us by firelight. When we ran out of kerosene she made a lamp out of a potato cut in half. It had a wick drawn through it, and it sat in a bowl of oil.

It was 1930, and we were living south of Gildford near the Hi-Line. Most of the farm families lived within a five-mile radius, and we sometimes after supper walked over to a neighbor's place, where we could buy a pail of milk for a nickel and some butter and eggs. It was a good excuse for getting out, and it gave Mama a chance to visit with another woman. One of the families owned, marvel of marvels, a radio. Every Wednesday night, from a Denver station, there was a continued story, a thriller that made our pulses race and stirred our imagination.

I remember so vividly holding Mama's hand and walking in the cold winter night, breathing in the clear, crisp air, enthralled as the moonlight turned the new snow into diamonds beneath our feet. Then, when we arrived, the extra wait while one of the big boys carried the battery in from the truck. They connected it up to the marvelous machine with all the skill and dexterity of a pair of brain surgeons. And then—that magic moment when the dial was turned on. We all sat breathless as the wonderful little box, amid squawks, crackles, and squeals, would begin where the story had left off the week before. My heart pounded in anticipation.

"John Worth . . . you will be shot . . . through the heart . . . at ten o'clock . . . tonight!" We sat mesmerized until the half hour was over. Then, dazed by the wonder of it all, we walked the three miles home to wait, to dream, for another week.

Imagine in this age of total mobility what it was like to be without any means of transportation. We seldom went far, but when we did, we walked. The only time we went to church or any other public gathering was when one of the farm families offered us a ride in the back of their grain truck. What a treat that was. The most memorable outing was riding the forty-five miles to Havre in the back of a truck with our five and two of the Anderson kids. Elmer, the oldest boy, fixed up a comfortable chair for Mama in the back of the truck, and we had a load. We brought quilts to sit on and packed a picnic lunch for our supper. Elmer played his guitar and we sang all the way to Havre.

Thirty miles an hour was as fast as that old truck could go, so it was a long ride. We were going to a revival meeting in Havre, held by the world famous Billy Sunday. Knute Anderson, father of the only Norwegian family in the community, was taking us at his wife's request. She didn't ask for much, but when she set her mind on something, she saw it through. Maybe she thought a touch of fire and brimstone might encourage him to give up some of his bad habits. He had other ideas.

Even though we weren't able to attend church regularly, we didn't lack for religious training. I don't remember a night when Mama didn't kneel beside the bed and give thanks for all our blessings. I had thought a lot about my chances of spending eternity in Heaven, and didn't think I could make it by just trying to be good, so I asked Mama if I ought to be baptized. She told me that I would know when the time came. It would have to be my decision.

It was a lovely balmy night as dusk approached. The stars began to shine like bits of crystal in the purple sky, and the air smelled of the pure, sweet scent of newly cut hay. It seemed a never-ending trip in the back of that truck, but when we passed the fairgrounds, on the outskirts of Havre, we knew we would soon be there.

Knute drove us to the Havre High School gymnasium and said he would be back to get us at half past ten. The immense crowd of people, all pushing and shoving to get a seat near the front, intimidated me, and I began to have second thoughts about going up to be baptized, but Billy said he would do it if I would. It looked as though we wouldn't even get a seat, let alone one near the front, and then some young men came with folding chairs, and we were seated in the front row.

Listening to Billy Sunday's thunderous message I knew for certain that I would never make it to Heaven on my own merits. If the reverend was God's messenger, he used some pretty strong words for his message. He clenched his fists and stomped his feet and made me tremble. "If you haven't been washed in the blood of the Lamb," he shouted, "you are nothing but weasel-eyed, pussy-footed, four-flushing, make-believe Christians!" And that was only the beginning.

When the time came for the altar call I was shaking, whether from fear or anticipation, I couldn't be sure. Mama was the first to stand up, and we all trooped after her. We were just about to kneel at the altar when I saw a well-worn deck of cards sticking out of my brother's back pocket. I had read somewhere that Baptists weren't partial to playing cards and decided it was up to me to get rid of the evidence. Just as I got my hand wedged in to get a grip on the cards, Billy started to kneel and my hand was trapped. I gave a yank, and the cards flew everywhere. Surely there couldn't have been only fifty-two cards in that deck. It looked more like a hundred, but nobody seemed to notice as we picked them up and stuffed them into our pockets.

With Billy Sunday right there close, everything else faded into the background. He moved so fast, touching each of us and shouting, "You are saved," or "you are healed," that he was almost a blur, but I felt the power surrounding that man in a way I haven't felt since.

There was a lot of hugging and sobbing and praise and glory before the revival meeting was over, but as we stood on the street waiting for Knute, I didn't feel any less sinful than I had before. It was already past the time that Knute had said he would be there, and we huddled together at the corner and waited, at first a little restlessly, but as the crowd melted away and we were the only ones left, we began to worry.

Finally, the truck came roaring around the corner, and Knute climbed out, staggered over to Elmer, gave him the keys, crawled into the back of the truck and began singing "Glory, Glory, Halleluiah." He sang it the whole thirty miles to Gildford.

By the time we got there, he was yelling that he needed a rest stop at the bar. Elmer went with him and came out a few minutes later with a Baby Ruth candy bar for each one of us kids. He told my brother later that he had taken all the money out of his Dad's pocket, and the bartender had promised not to give him a drink.

Knute came out mumbling that he'd take his business elsewhere in the future, and we headed for home. That night would always have a special place in my memory, first for my baptism at the fire and brimstone revival meeting, but almost as much for the candy bar. It was the first time in my life that I had ever had a candy bar all to myself.

Leah

My religious period caused me no little anxiety that year. I thought I could be good without trying so hard after being baptized, but it seemed I had to try all the harder. I was still troubled about my sins. I had found a book in the school library about the seven deadly sins: anger, gluttony, pride, envy, greed, lust, and sloth. I was surely guilty of all of them except maybe sloth and lust, and I didn't know what those words meant. Sloth, I discovered, was laziness. Yes, I had that one all right, but lust wasn't in my vocabulary. It was a heavy load for twelve-year-old girl to carry.

That year Billy and I walked miles, weather permitting, and we found a new friend on one of our Saturday tramps across the countryside. We had passed this farmhouse before, but Billy said a strange foreign couple lived there, and we weren't to stop. This only served to pique my curiosity, and I insisted one day that I had a horrible headache and couldn't wait until we got home. We stopped at the mailbox that said "Pappas" on the side. Billy was dragging his feet, but I went ahead. I had knocked on the door by the time he caught up with me. I knocked, waited, and then knocked again and was just about to leave when the door opened and we were enveloped in a scent so exotic that it has stayed with me to this day.

"Please to come in," the woman said. She was plump, with rosy dark skin and slanted eyes, and she spoke in a fruity voice made even more memorable by her accent. I was enchanted. When Billy told her that I had a headache and needed an aspirin, she gave me a thoughtful look. "No aspirin, no aspirin," she said, "but come in and I will cure her headache." She led me over to a couch where there was a scattering of the *True Story* magazines she had been reading. The couch was also covered with beautiful scarves, and incense was burning in a little holder.

She had a ring on every finger, and her hair was black and shiny as coal. Her lips were red, and she had blue eye shadow on her eyelids. I wondered if she had seen us coming and put the make-up on just for us or if she had been expecting company. I don't know about Billy, but she surely made an impression on me.

She drew me between her knees and, grasping my head between her fat little hands, placed a thumb on the back of my neck and gave it a twist. I was sure my neck was broken. "You will have no more headaches now," she said, and winked at me.

Then, pushing aside the stack of *True Story* magazines, she pulled me up on the couch beside her. "Here, have a chocolate," she said. The biggest box of chocolates I had ever seen was sitting on a stand, and I don't know what fascinated me the most, the *True Stories* or the chocolates. One of the eighth-grade girls had brought a *True Story* to school, and I had heard Mama scolding her, so I knew she wouldn't approve of my new friend. She told us her name was Leah and that she had met her husband in the big war. She and her husband had not been blessed with children, she said, and she was very lonely for her relatives in Greece. She cried many tears, but her husband loved her very much, and so she could not leave him. Here was a ready-made *True Story* with enough romance to stir my twelve-year-old imagination.

When Billy said it was time to go she hugged us both and begged us to come and visit her again. Then she said to me, "I see you have big eyes for my magazines. Take one for yourself, and the next time you come, you can trade it for another one." I saw that Billy was shaking his head, but I didn't want to hurt her feelings. At least that was what I told myself as I hotfooted it home. I hid in the back of the coal shed the next day and read all about the poor girls who had been betrayed by the "passions of lust." I didn't quite know what that meant, but I certainly intended to find out. I knew that "everything went black," and in due time some of these girls would have to confess to their parents that they were in trouble and would be forced to leave home.

I could hardly wait to get another magazine, and we went

back several times before the winter weather made it impossible, but I had learned a lot by then. I liked Leah more every time I saw her and wanted to be just like her. I sent away for samples of Tangee lipstick and mascara and practiced outlining my eyes and lips and tried to make my voice like hers. The *Colliers* magazine and the *Saturday Evening Post* had coupons for free samples, usually O-do-ro-no and toothpaste or Ivory soap, but sometimes for mascara and lipstick. Our aunt in Minneapolis sent us her old magazines along with our cousins' outgrown clothes, and we were always thrilled when the box came in the mail. We clipped the coupons, pasted a three-cent stamp on the envelope, and waited for the little packages to arrive.

A little knowledge is a dangerous thing, and with my flair for the dramatic, I convinced myself that soon I, too, was destined to disgrace my family. I was just entering pre-puberty, and my stomach was getting puffy, and although I hadn't the slightest idea how I could have gotten into this interesting condition, I went through agonies of guilt that winter. I wished fervently then that I could go to confession in a dark little booth that smelled of wine and furniture polish the way my cousins did. They had solemnly assured me the summer we were in Great Falls that if we would just become Catholic, we would never have to worry about our sins again.

Papa's Visit

It was a rainy afternoon in April 1927, and the weather had turned cold. We were looking forward to a game of dominoes after supper, and Billy and I were just bringing in the wood and coal when we saw a man walking up the road with a large pack on his back. When we ran in with the news, Mama turned pale. "Oh merciful heavens," she almost whispered, "It's Will. I know it's Will."

When the door burst open without the courtesy of a knock and a man came in, the walls seemed to shrink. "Kids, I'm home," he said, as he stood there with his arms outstretched while we looked at Mama for a clue as to how we should act.

"Shut the door, Will," Mama said. "Children, this is your father."

I suppose he must have been considered handsome with his dark eyes and thick black hair. To me he was only a shadow figure, a stranger.

"So here you are, my pretty little girls." He opened his arms again, turning to include us, while Billy made a face and crossed his eyes behind Papa's back. Mama fixed him something to eat, and he soon had Donna and Bette sitting on his lap and going through his pockets looking for candy.

I was nine that year, short and skinny, and wishing I had at least inherited his good looks. We sure didn't get much else from him. I resented his intrusion into our lives. We were getting along just fine, I thought, and I hoped his visit would be a short one. Where had he been the summer Mama was so sick? Where had he been when she didn't have money to pay for the winter coal?

That night Papa told stories of the places he had seen in his travels, with him always the hero, entertaining the family until bedtime. Then, looking around, he said, "Only one bed? You all must be pretty crowded."

Mama gave him a level glance and said, "We are. The two older girls will sleep in the schoolhouse and the two little girls will sleep with me, and you can fix a palette on the floor beside the stove in the schoolhouse. I imagine it will be better than sleeping in a boxcar, or wherever you've slept since we saw you last."

"You're a cold-hearted woman, Delia," he said. "You don't know what it's like out there. There were times I almost couldn't keep body and soul together. Why, I could tell you stories that would break your heart."

"I'm sure you could, Will. You always did have that ability. Now it has been a long day, and we're all tired." She began to pull her hair from the knot on top of her head and brush and braid it over her shoulder.

"Remember how I used to do that for you, Deely?" he said, and then, giving her a doleful look, he picked up the lantern. "Come on, kids, it looks like we're going to be together for a while. We might as well start getting acquainted!"

It was a dreadful week, with Mama scarcely ever smiling. Papa made half-hearted efforts at starting conversations with Billy and me, but soon gave up and found a book to read. There were muffled arguments every day, and he was getting edgy and mean. Once I was whirling around on the piano stool when Billy pulled it out from under me. I fell hard on my seat and began bawling at the top of my lungs. Papa jumped up and started hitting him with his fists, all the time telling him that he should never hurt a little girl like that, as she might not be able to have babies when she grew up. Billy had bruises all over his back and arms the next day, and I felt awful about being the cause of it. I disliked Papa even more after that.

"I want all you kids to clear out of here," Papa said one evening. "Your Mother and I are going to have a little talk. In fact, you can all sleep in the schoolhouse tonight."

Mama jumped up so fast she knocked her chair over. "Children, you stay right here. Will, you and I have nothing to talk about."

He walked around the table and placed his large hand on the back of her neck and squeezed. "Remember the last time you shut me out, Delia? Remember? Have it your way. They can stay or go, but you and I are going to have our little talk."

"Then we'll stay," Billy said.

"Is that what you want, Delia?"

Mama seemed to wilt. "No, children, go. Do as he says."

A widow lady by the name of Hester Hammond farmed alone with her fourteen-year-old son, and she needed help butchering several pigs, since her son had sprained his wrist. Papa volunteered and did some other chores around their place in exchange for some of the meat. We were so looking forward to eating that quarter of pork. We had it hanging in the lean-to wrapped in cloth when Papa left, his clothes mended and a package of roast pork sandwiches in his backpack. It was almost a nice enough gift to make me feel better about Papa. That was the last time I remember seeing him until I was a grown woman with children of my own.

We never did get the pork after all. There was a family in the community who depended entirely upon their wheat crops. Unlike other farmers who raised a few livestock and some poultry, milked a cow, and sold cream and butter, Mr. Adams had announced several times that he disdained such slavery. But after a series of crop failures his children came to school with lard on their bread, cardboard in their shoes, and holes in their socks the size of quarters. One morning our pork was gone. The Adams kids came to school the next day with pork sandwiches.

"They must need it more than we do," Mama said. "So don't say a word to them. I feel so sorry for those poor children." Those poor children were eating our pork.

We had two weeks of school left when Mrs. Hammond invited us over for dinner. I was listening around the door as usual and heard Mama crying. Mrs. Hammond was patting her on the back, and saying, "Are you sure?" When Mama nodded, she continued. "Well, I'll see to it that you are hired back next year. I'm not on the school board for nothing. You at least ought to know where you're going to be when the new one gets here. Damn the men! I've never met an unselfish one yet. I might be able to talk the rest of the school board into letting you stay here for the summer, too. I could use some help with the garden, and I know of some others who need help, too. I can't guarantee it, mind you, but I'll see what can be done." A week later the school board had their meeting and brought next year's contract for Mama to sign.

After a long wet spring, the sun dried the puddles in the schoolyard and Mrs. Hammond told Mama there was a pretty good chance that we would be allowed to stay for the summer months. Mama was still sick a lot of the time and went to bed right after dismissing school each day. Billy and I were in charge, and we cooked something for the kids, but Mama couldn't eat much. Nevertheless, it was a happy time for all of us, with the pastures green and the pink and yellow cactus blooming. We found birds' nests, and johnny jump-ups and yellow bells wherever we walked.

Jimmy Walker was Billy's age, and they had become good friends. Billy often stayed overnight with him, and I was no longer his best buddy. I resented it. One day I heard the two boys talking about camping out all night and cooking their dinner over a bonfire. I threatened to tell Mama, but they convinced me it was only a joke. I should have told anyway.

The next Saturday evening was balmy and warm, and I was grouchy because Billy was staying overnight with Jimmy. Mama was teaching us girls to darn socks to keep us occupied when we heard the sound of wagon wheels and the drumming of horses' hooves. When we opened the door, we could smell smoke, and Mr. Walker was yelling, "Prairie fire . . . Prairie fire! Get in the wagon!" We could see a rim of fire just over the hill. We sat in the wagon and waited, ready to race if the fire came at us. We saw two plows making a firebreak at the top of the hill, and as we watched, the fire seemed to be burning itself out. Thank God for the rainy spring.

"I think I know how this fire got started," Walker said, "and two boys are going to get their hind-ends blistered. One of 'em is Billy Hanson, and the other one is that fool kid of mine. Have you ever seen a prairie fire that couldn't be stopped? Have you?" He glared at Mama. "Well I have, and I aim to get those kids and teach 'em a lesson. Are you coming with me?"

Mama was so pale I thought she was going to faint, but she spoke right up to him. "I'm perfectly capable of punishing my own child, and you can be sure that I will make a thorough job of it."

Mama said I should go with him, and we sped off. I had never seen a wagon go so fast, as Mr. Walker lashed the horses again and again. I was crying by the time we got to Walkers' place, crying for the horses and crying for Mama and the two scared white-faced kids waiting by the barn.

Mr. Walker looked at Jimmy and pointed to the house yelling "Git," and that kid moved, and he moved fast. I scrambled out of the wagon as he grabbed Billy by the seat of his pants and kicked him as though he were a football. He lit running and I was right behind him.

"And don't come back here again!" he roared.

We didn't say a word to each other, and it was dark by the time we ran the two miles home. When Billy and I came in the door, Mama pointed to the razor strop that Papa had left hanging on the wall. He walked over to the bed and handed it to her. I can still see the lamplight flickering against the window, hear the awful swish of the razor strop, and see Mama's pale arm rising again and again from the bed as she counted, "eight . . . nine . . . ten," and then buried her head in the pillow and cried as if her heart would break. She could have beaten him a hundred times, and it wouldn't have hurt as much as seeing her cry.

The next day Mrs. Hammond drove up in her buggy. She had a solemn look on her face, and we knew she had bad news. "You

have the job for next year. They can't take that away from you,"
she said, "but they won't agree to letting you stay here for the
summer. Walker was the hardest to convince. He wanted to have
your contract revoked!"

Mama nodded. "I'm not surprised, but he did have a good
reason," she said.

"Pish and tosh! Men always think they have a good reason
for the things they do to us." Mrs. Hammond's eyes sparked fire.
"But," she brightened, "I hear there's going to be a new bakery
in town, and you do have a light touch with piecrust. I'll take
you to town as soon as you're feeling up to it."

Mama nodded. "I could do that. We can make it through the
summer just fine. After all, as you can plainly see, this isn't the
first time."

Mama got the job at the bakery, found a little house to rent in
Big Sandy for the summer, and soon Billy was working at odd
jobs and I was tagging along, helping out when I could. We often
stayed over and helped with the haying and shocking. One of the
families we worked for had a French-sounding name and spoke
with a pronounced accent. There was an air of mystery about
their place that fueled my ever-present curiosity. The barnyard
had a little creek running through it and a small building made
of rocks sitting on the edge of the water. It was kept locked and
the kids would clam up when we asked them what it was for.
They told us we were supposed to stay away from it and stop
asking questions. Billy had suspicions. He said he heard the clink
of bottles and low men's voices and cars in the yard during the
night on several occasions when he slept over. We had heard of
Prohibition, but it didn't touch our lives, so it didn't occur to us
that something illegal was going on. In later years, my brother
visited the family and asked one of the girls, now a gray-haired
woman, if what he suspected was true.

She just smiled.

"What do you think?" she asked.

There was a single woman who ran the biggest cattle ranch in the area. She had come out from the East, homesteaded by herself, and had withstood the cold winters, the dry summers, and the loneliness. She had quietly moved in and bought more land for a pittance as others gave up and moved on. I admired Penelope for her independence. She always wore bib overalls and smoked a corncob pipe, which I thought very devilish and clever of her. She hired only women when she needed help, and the community wives and daughters were glad to earn a little extra money. They would leave lunches prepared at home for their men and spend the day at Penelope Frazier's ranch, where lunch consisted of roast beef, bread, and coffee.

I was thrilled to be hired for haying that summer. My job was to help fork the hay into the hayloft. The second day I managed to stick a pitchfork clear through my foot. Penelope snorted as she jerked it out. It didn't even bleed much, and I begged to be allowed to continue working. She poured Lysol over my foot, tied it up in a dishtowel, and told me to stay out of the way. She didn't want anyone working for her who was stupid enough to stick a pitchfork through her foot. I thought it was very mean-spirited of her.

Summer was over all too soon, as summers have a way of doing, and school began in September. When winter arrived, it came with a vengeance. The community was prepared for cold weather, the fur robes were brought out of storage, and runners replaced the wagon wheels. It was a thrill when we got a chance to ride in the sleigh, our breath making icicles in the scarves wrapped around our chins.

Then the days came when Mama could hardly get out of bed in the mornings. Billy and I got up early and started the fire in the schoolhouse each day and helped as much as we could. One night we were wakened and hustled off in a sleigh. We wrapped the fur robes around us and rested our feet on hot bricks as we raced through the night. My heart pounded, and the breath froze in my throat. I listened to the whispers in the dimly lit bedroom with the thick quilts turned back, and watched while a tin bed warmer was whisked over the sheets, and then snuggled down with my sisters into a strange soft bed.

Curious as usual, I sensed that this wasn't the time for asking questions. We went back to sleep to the smell of fresh sheets and newly washed wooden floors. The next morning we were given a breakfast of ham and eggs and pancakes, and we ate until we were stuffed. Then we were taken to the teacherage for a "surprise."

Our new little sister was named Harriet, we were told, and we were allowed to hold her. She felt like a kitten squirming against my chest, and I had a lump in my throat that I couldn't swallow. I cried when I had to give her back to Mama. We stayed at the neighbor's place for a few days, and when we went back to school, it was as though nothing had happened. Mama was up and dressed and ready for school, and the baby wasn't there. Hester Hammond had kindly offered to take her until Mama could care for her at home.

When we talked about going to see the baby, Mrs. Hammond said she had other plans, and we would have to come some other time. When spring came and it was time to move on, Mrs. Hammond persuaded Mama to leave little Hattie with her a while longer, just until we got settled. Letters were exchanged. Then Mama wrote, saying that she had a good job for the next year and would come and get Harriet the last week in August. We were excited at the idea of having the baby back with us and counted the days. We watched the mail and waited, but no letter came. When Mama wrote to the Walkers, she got a letter right back. Mrs. Hammond had sold her farm and departed bag and baggage. She had left no forwarding address.

I didn't meet my sister again until thirty years later, when I was living in Hingham on the Hi-Line. Harriet was living in Portland, Oregon. She was going to be in Great Falls for a bowling tournament, and I decided to drive over to see her. I worried for weeks. Would she like me? Would I like her? Would I even know her when I saw her?

I found the Holiday Inn and parked my car. Breathing hard, I found her room and stood there with my fist raised, ready to knock, when the door opened. Four pairs of eyes looked at me. Two of the women were short with brown hair. She must be one of these, I thought. Then a tall, big-boned blonde stepped forward.

"I'm Harriet. Are you my sister?"

She was very pretty, and the other women told me she was the best bowler on their team. We eyed each other but couldn't start up much of a conversation with everyone bustling around getting ready to leave for the bowling alley. It was like that the rest of the day, and I drove the hundred miles home feeling depressed and disappointed.

The next time I saw Harriet was twelve years later, when my husband and I drove with Maribelle and her husband to Portland to Harriet's daughter's wedding. Harriet was more beautiful than the bride even though she was on oxygen and in a wheelchair. They had a big outdoor party with champagne and an orchestra. Three months later, we were notified: Harriet had died of cancer.

Perpetual Motion

From the moment we turned in the gate of the Black Coulee School near the Bear's Paw Mountains, we knew it was going to be a special place. There was a hayfield just beyond the schoolyard fence, and the buildings were nestled at the foot of gentle pine-covered hills, an easy climb for adventurous kids. The teacherage was a log building with a separate bedroom, an unheard of luxury. The spacious kitchen-living room held a big round table and chairs and a big kitchen range. Billy and I sat behind it and played rummy when it was too cold to play outside, and the memory warms me even now.

The schoolhouse itself had a new coat of white paint, and the inside was scrubbed like a church. There was a belfry on top with a big iron bell. It had a no-nonsense ring that pealed out the start of the school day, recess, and the noon hour. Being chosen as the bell ringer for the week was a special reward for good behavior. This was clearly a place to live up to.

Almost every year Mama went to Great Falls to the teachers' convention. Usually we were invited to stay with some of the school patrons, but this year Maribelle was coming out from Big Sandy to stay with us. She wouldn't be there until late the next afternoon, though, and Billy would be in charge for a night and a day.

Before the dust had cleared away behind the truck taking Mama to town, Billy revealed his plan for an adventure. He had a huge secret to tell me, he said, and headed for the schoolhouse. He propped a makeshift ladder against the wall, got a foothold, and began to climb up into the belfry, with me clinging to his pant leg. I was, and still am, a devout coward about heights, but I perched on the ledge up there while he pulled out a brown envelope from its hiding place. "In here," he said, tapping the envelope, "are sketches that will revolutionize the world. It's a perpetual motion machine, and I invented it. We won't need any gas or coal, and the big oil companies and the mine owners will give anything to keep this invention from the rest of the world. Now that they know we're alone tonight, they'll make their move." Billy could be very convincing. I was scared enough to go along with any plan he had.

After supper he told us some more of his ongoing story about the wonderful ranch in Colorado where we would live after he got the patent on his invention. After the girls were asleep, Billy said, "I know they're out there, and you'll just have to leave things in my hands. They could kidnap the little kids to make me tell them where the plans are, or they might torture you and me. You can't tell what people will do when they're desperate." We kept the fire going and promised each other that we would stay awake. We had our feet on the oven door as we began to doze, and I woke up from a dream of being held prisoner in an ice cave. The oven was cold and the room was even colder. Billy was shaking me.

"It's time," he said. "We have to get the girls into their coats. Now here's the plan. We'll slip out of this side window and crawl across the yard and under the fence to the haystack. Don't make any noise."

The kids balked at being wakened out of a sound sleep, and by this time I was beginning to doubt the wisdom of my genius brother myself. After all, we were just kids. The enemy could come and get us any time they wanted to. Our hands and clothes were full of thistles when we got to the haystack. At first it felt good snuggling down in the sweet-smelling hay, but soon the cold began to seep through our coats and blankets, and we couldn't get comfortable no matter which way we turned. By morning we were all stiff and cold, and not even Billy could keep us from a warm stove and food. Billy started the fire, and when I was slicing bread and reaching for the butter, he snatched it out of my hands.

"Don't you know that butter is the easiest thing in the world to poison?" he demanded. My mouth watered as he scraped it into the fire.

Then I got a jar of Mama's grape jelly down from the cupboard, but he grabbed that, too. "See those black specks?" he said. "They're probably lead poisoning."

By the time Maribelle got there he had opened every jar and scraped the jam over the fence into the pasture, and the flies were having a picnic. She was horrified. "Mama worked all one Saturday making that jelly, to say nothing of the cost of the grapes and sugar!" she shrieked. "She's going to whip the daylights out of you."

Billy just stared at the empty jars. "You'll all thank me when you realize I just saved the whole family from a horrible death."

Mama was heartsick about the jam, and Billy knew the air rifle he wanted so badly would be a long time coming now. All of us girls, including me, his biggest fan, grumbled when we had to eat plain toast for breakfast that winter.

"You'll be talking out of the other side of your mouths when we get our ranch and I'm a famous inventor," Billy said.

Boughs of Folly

E very year when the Sears catalog arrived in the mail, it was like a letter from an old friend. We called it the Christmas book, and it provided entertainment for us during the dark days of winter. Billy had nearly worn out the page that showed the air rifle he wanted. Once or twice a year we sent away an order, and each of us had a special request. Mama let us order a ukulele one Christmas. I can't imagine how we talked her into it, but Billy and I both had blisters on our fingers from practicing the chords when she regretfully told us she had to send it back. It was a bitter disappointment. I thought we were finally going to have some music in our lives, and I still feel deprived, but she needed the money to help pay the grocery bill, and that was all there was to it.

My sisters and I cut out the best models from the catalog and pasted them on cardboard to use as paper dolls, designing fabulous dresses and hats and naming them after our favorite movie stars, Clara Bow, Jean Harlow, and Bette Davis. After we had extracted the last bit of make-believe from that book it was torn in half and strung on wires and hung in the outhouses. The back part with the guns and tools was hung in the "his" and the part containing the women's unmentionables was hung in the "hers."

On warm October days we could ask to "leave the room" and steal a little time from our lessons to sit on that sun-warmed toilet seat and maybe choose something wonderful to wish for. The little outhouses wouldn't be so welcoming when the snow started to fly. The snow would build up in the corners of the seat and block the door with ice, and we would sit on our hands to keep from freezing our bottoms.

Each year we hoped that this was the Christmas we would get a coveted bit of frivolous junk instead of the usual caps and mittens and new flannel pajamas that Mama sat up nights making for us. When I was eleven, and we were living about ten miles from Two Dot at the Olaf School in the beautiful Little Belt Mountains, we did. I'm not sure how Mama came by the extra money for Christmas that year, but I think she furnished the lunches for one of the card parties, and charged twenty-five cents a plate, just to give us this one wonderful Christmas.

Mama went to the teacher's convention again that year, and I remember waiting breathlessly for her return. I sat up in the branches of a big tree and watched for the truck. There were patches of ice in the yard, and I shivered as I clung to the tree branch until I saw the truck creeping over the hill. I wanted to be the first one to greet her, and I skinned down that tree, hit the ground running, slipped on a patch of ice, and fell on my wrist, spraining it. I bellowed with pain as Mama climbed down from the truck. I enjoyed being fussed over and milked it for all it was worth. I couldn't help wash the dishes with my swollen and bandaged wrist, nor take my turn at the scrub board on washday—too bad.

Mama was smiling and happy as she told us that we were going to have a special Christmas this year. She hadn't wrapped the packages yet, she said, so we were on our honor not to go looking for them. We all promised, but every time I was in the schoolhouse by myself the temptation was like another presence in the room. After all, I deserved a special surprise. Hadn't I been in pain all this time with my sprained wrist? I couldn't even tie my shoelaces. If I just happened upon the presents, then it wouldn't be my fault, would it? I wasn't really looking, I told myself, but something seemed to lead me to a door under the basement stairs.

My conscience said "don't look," but my curiosity urged me to take just a tiny peek. I grabbed the door handle and gave it a jerk. It wouldn't budge. I tried to look through the keyhole, but it was too dark to see. In my mind's eye I saw Mama's key ring in the top right-hand drawer of her desk. I raced up the stairs, grabbed the keys, and hurried down. The first one I tried turned the lock, and I hesitated. Did I really want to do this? The door made a sound like fingernails on a blackboard as I slowly opened it, sure I would be caught. There before me were more toys than I had ever seen in one place. I really only noticed two things, a set of aluminum cooking pans, little girl size, and a beautiful doll with blue eyes and long curly golden hair. I knew—knew, with all the self-centered passion of a child—that my mother would never have bought that doll for anyone but me. I shut the door, listening for footsteps as I sneaked away and returned the key to its place.

My heart was heavy all that Christmas season. For two weeks I ate my food without tasting it and slept, haunted by dreams of sneering Santa Clauses and iron-barred doors slamming shut. They say a criminal always returns to the scene of the crime, and I was relieved to see that everything had been moved when I opened that door once again. I went through all the holiday motions, helping to trim the tree, popping and stringing popcorn and cranberries, though my heart wasn't in it.

When Christmas Eve finally arrived I sleepwalked through the pageant and forgot my lines in the school play. The final humiliation came when right there in the middle of the stage my garter broke and my stocking slid slowly down my leg, coming to rest on my shoe, looking like a wet rat. I stood there red-faced listening to the snorts and giggles coming from the audience and thought it was probably just punishment for spoiling Mama's surprise. The next morning Mama was all smiles when she brought the presents out. I was crestfallen in the light of her beaming face as I exclaimed falsely over the set of cooking pans and watched my sister Donna unwrap the beautiful golden-haired blue-eyed doll.

She was ecstatic. "Oh, she's beautiful," she said. "I'm going to name her Gloria." And in all these years I've never met a Gloria I could like.

The Great Mail Robbery

It was the year of the porcupine. The long, lazy fall days were over, the anticipation of the holidays was behind us, and we were getting restless. The only thing that kept the big boys from open rebellion was reading time. Mama's favorite authors were Zane Grey and B. M. Bower, with their rustlers, hold-up men, and other outlaws, and the kids loved it. Any other free time was spent drilling the eighth graders for the county exams in the spring. Mama could see that there were some fine minds going to waste, and she deeply felt the need for giving at least some of them a chance at higher learning.

It promised to be a long dull winter, with little sunshine to relieve our gray world. The acrid smell of mittens drying by the stove, stale lunch boxes, chalk, and unwashed bodies had replaced the smell of fresh air and drying leaves, hayfields, and ripened wheat. Billy hadn't forgotten about the air rifle he wanted. He knew Mama didn't have the extra money, but he had a plan for earning it himself. The price was etched on his mind: $2.95, plus postage.

He had borrowed some traps from a bachelor farmer, and with the county paying twenty-five cents a rabbit pelt, he would have the money in no time, he thought. He was wrong. Before we got the traps set out, a howling blizzard hit during the night. The wind blew the snow into six-foot drifts, and the temperature dropped to twenty below zero. Although I was Billy's trusty sidekick, I couldn't be persuaded to go out with him in such cold. Even the rabbits knew better. We wouldn't be able to set the traps until there was a break in the weather. Finally, early in March, a chinook wind blew in, and the snowdrifts melted to puddles, the wind softened, and the air smelled of spring. Billy's luck turned with the weather, and it seemed rabbits were everywhere.

By April 1 Billy had sold his pelts and sent off his order. He could hardly contain himself until the day the long package came in the mail. The air rifle was beautiful, with the polished wooden stock gleaming in the lamplight.

"One thing I must insist on," Mama said, "is that you never—and I mean never—take this gun outside when any of the school-children are in the yard."

Billy's face fell. He had dreamed of putting ol' Blackie in his place, but he did promise, although I think he must have crossed his fingers behind his back. He kept his secret for a whole week, but he just had to tell someone. He swore his best friend to secrecy hope to die and rot in your tracks if he told anyone else, but his friend was fickle.

The next day at recess Blackie pushed Billy around the corner of the schoolhouse where Mama couldn't see.

"Hey, kid, I hear you've got a gun."

Billy looked down and said nothing.

"Ain't you too young to have a gun, squirt?"

"It's just an air rifle, and it won't kill anyone," Billy said.

"You're a little liar," Blackie sneered, and soon all the boys had taken up the chant.

"I'm not lyin' and I'd show it to you, but Mama made me promise not to take it out when any of you kids were in the schoolyard." Billy was furious.

"Okay, then, if you're tellin' the truth you could take it down to the mailbox at last recess, that isn't in the schoolyard."

Billy was hurt to the quick. "I'm not a liar and I'll prove it!"

Blackie looked mean. "I still think you're lyin', and if you don't show up with that gun I'm gonna trounce you good!"

Last recess was upon him. Billy walked across the schoolyard, grabbed the gun from under the bed, and raced for the mailbox just as the mailman came over the hill. Almost before he had skidded to a stop, Blackie jerked the gun out of his hands.

"Alright, you guys, get your bandanas on. Here he comes!"

They were all standing in the road, faces covered, when the mailman pulled to a stop.

"What in THUNDER are you kids up to?" he roared.

"Reach for the sky, mister, and hand over them mail bags." Blackie hoisted the gun to his shoulder and aimed. The mailman floored the gas pedal, and the gang scattered, but not before a pellet had pierced the isinglass windshield and nicked the mailman's nose. He wheeled the Model T around and headed for town as the gang raced for the schoolhouse. The gun was hastily passed back to Billy, and he ran for the teacherage, put it back under the bed, and walked slowly back to the schoolhouse. There was going to be trouble, and he was right in the middle of it.

An hour later, the mailman, with a bandage on his nose, and two members of the school board, one of them Blackie's father, filed solemnly into the schoolroom and told their story.

"Well," Mama said, "We'll get to the bottom of this right now. All those who had anything to do with this . . . this . . . business, raise your hands!" It didn't work this time. She was met with silence.

"Who's gun was it?"

"Billy Hanson gave it to us," one of the little kids said.

"No, I didn't give it to them," Billy began, "but . . ."

"Was it your gun?" one of the fathers asked.

"Yes, but . . ."

"Get it and bring it to me, and then I want you," pointing to Blackie, "to tell us what happened."

Blackie twisted and squirmed. "Well, you see, Billy here, he got a new rifle, and . . . uh . . . he thought it would be a good joke to . . . uh . . . hold up the mailman—just for fun and all."

"Now wait a minute," the mailman interrupted. "The guy that pulled that trigger was a lot bigger than Billy Hanson and had a voice just like yours."

"The jig's up, kid," Blackie's father said. "You can't lie your way out of this one."

They looked at each other while the big clock ticked on, and it was Blackie who looked away first.

"Okay, we done it. But it was only a joke," he mumbled.

"You think this is a joke?" the mailman said, pointing to his nose. "By golly, if this township had a sheriff you'd be sitting in jail right now!"

"You'd better get at your books, Blackie, and try to learn what this fine lady is teaching you, or reform school will be the only college you'll be going to. We're gonna take your gun for a week or two, kid, but the rest of you honyockers are in this up to your necks. And Blackie's in deeper than the others," Blackie's father said.

Blackie had to mop the schoolhouse floor every week, and the others were chopping wood the rest of the school term—and this was after their lickings.

When Mama switched from Zane Grey to *Tom Sawyer* and *Huckleberry Finn*, the kids all groaned, but by May 1 they were talking about building rafts and exploring caves. The entire eighth grade passed their exams in the spring, and some of them went on to high school and college. One of them practiced law for many years in Montana.

They don't call him Blackie anymore.

Awards Night

School had already started, but we hadn't yet settled on the one we would attend. Mama had taken a job cooking at Melvin Tew's ranch south of Gildford that summer. We all worked planting and weeding a big garden. Billy drove the tractor, and my job was herding the cows on horseback. I loved that job. What twelve-year-old girl wouldn't? We stayed on at the Tew's, getting our things packed and ready to go, while Billy started school in Hingham and got a job at the Kersey Hotel.

It was awards night, an event I had been looking forward to for weeks. Billy was a sophomore in Hingham, and he was to be awarded some trophies for track. He had won first in the mile at the Hill County meet. He wanted Mama to attend the awards ceremony and had invited me, too. I had a new dress, made on Mama's trusty Singer, but my hair was a problem. It was dry, sun-bleached, and straight. I thought that if I could just get it to curl, I would be transformed. Mama told me how they curled their hair when she was a girl. They wrapped strands of wet hair around strips of cloth, tied it up in knots and left it all day to dry. I agreed to try it.

We tore a dishtowel into strips, and Mama went to work. When she was finished I walked around all day with my hair in rags. Then, in my new dress and polished shoes, I watched as Mama unwrapped my hair. It sprang into wiry curls—lots and lots of curls that stood out from my scalp like the snakes on the head of Medusa. It wasn't bad enough that I had knobby knees and was just generally awkward, now I had a bushy head of hair that couldn't be tamed. No matter how we brushed and combed, my hair had a mind of its own. There wasn't much we could do with it. If we wet it, that would just make it worse, so Mama made a ribbon out of the leftover material from my dress and tied my hair back with a big bow. I looked like I had just stepped out of the pages of *Rebecca of Sunnybrook Farm*.

Mr. Tew arrived in the truck to take us to the awards ceremony. I sulked all the way to town. Since we had been invited to dinner, we drove directly to the hotel. I was beginning to get nervous, sure that everyone would be looking at me and would see all my flaws immediately. But when Billy introduced us to a beautiful white-haired lady I felt transformed. She put her arms around me. "So here's the pretty sister that Billy has been talking about. How sweet you look with the ribbon matching your dress." And then she hugged Mama, too, and told her how much they thought of Billy and said how proud she must be. She was my friend that instant, and as it turned out we would be friends for the rest of our lives.

Ida Kersey and her husband had come out to the Hi-Line to homestead, as had so many other couples, but when he had a heart attack they knew they had to give up the homestead and start looking for some other way to make a living. They moved to town, where he managed a dairy business. The county was building a road, and Ida ran the cook car for the workers. Then she leased the local hotel, and she became famous for her doughnuts and excellent meals. When they heard the hotel was up for sale, Ida persuaded her husband to borrow the money for the down payment. She was sure that her future was here on the prairie. Hadn't Haley's Comet been streaking across the sky the very night they stepped off the train? And she did make a go of it, doing the work of two people and taking care of her husband. She never seemed to run out of energy, and she was the kindest person I ever met.

That night of the awards ceremony Mama and I had seats near the stage, and when we walked in with our new friend I forgot my awkwardness and my fuzzy hair. Mrs. Kersey had given my self-confidence a lift that bolstered me in the difficult year ahead.

By 1930 school consolidation had led to the closing of some of the smaller country schools, and Mama was among those teachers who lost their jobs. Consolidation was an ugly word for teachers like my mother. The country was in the deepest part of the Depression, and closing down some of the smaller schools was simply good economics. For the first time Mama was jobless, and we were flat broke and didn't know how we were going to make it through the winter. Mama contacted the county superintendent and found a solution. The county paid the school district for each child enrolled for the school term, and since there were five of us, the trustees of the school, short of cash and students, found us a house in Gildford.

Gildford was one of the many little villages in Montana along the Great Northern track. The railroad cut through so as to almost shove the town onto the highway. You had to cross the tracks to get to Main Street. From there the streets dribbled off toward the post office, the barbershop, and a Mom and Pop store. There was a hardware store and a flourmill in that little town. The farmers brought sacks of wheat to be ground for the winter's supply of flour, and the mill did a flourishing business. All the streets leading to the two-story brick schoolhouse were worn and dusty. But the flag waved proudly in front of the building every school day; the schoolhouse was the town's main building, and it was a structure the residents were proud of.

Living in town would be a drastic change for us. We had never associated much with the kids in the schools where Mama taught. Maybe it was because we had each other and were satisfied with our own company. It didn't worry me, as I was sure I would make friends, and if not, we would just continue as we had been.

Along with many other families on the Hi-Line and beyond we would make it through that winter on relief. None of us liked the word, but we would have been hungry a lot of the time without it. The commodities kept us fed, and we had just enough money for the house rent and the heat and lights. We were given butter and dried fruit, beans and rice, and lots of oranges, a treat that we had seldom enjoyed in our country living.

Maribelle had been living in Deer Lodge with my father's sister Clara and her family, working for her board and room, and although my aunt was an unpleasant woman who worked her hard, she didn't want to come back. She had made friends there and had hopes for a scholarship. She had her future all mapped out, but she had to come. She was part of the deal. Five children, Mama had promised, and five was what they were going to get. My sixteen-year-old sister was pretty hard to get along with that winter. She appointed herself head housekeeper, and she was a tough taskmaster. If we came home with muddy shoes or torn clothes, we were sure to get a tongue-lashing.

This was the first time Mama hadn't had to work, and she made the most of it. When there was anything going on at the town hall she was the first to offer to help decorate, the first to be there with a batch of cookies, and always among the clean-up crew. She never missed a P.T.A. meeting. She quilted with the ladies to make blankets for the needy, and she brought her wonderful pies to all the church suppers. She learned how to play bridge that winter and came home with a pocketful of quarters twice a week. She was having such a good time that I sat up and waited when she played cards in the evening, just to see that shine on her face when she came home.

We were within walking distance of a church for the first time, too, and we attended faithfully. Still, I watched Mama's glow fade little by little. The good ladies of the town had circled their wagons, and they weren't letting her in. She had five children with no husband in sight, and they had decided she couldn't be trusted.

We had lived all our lives in the quiet of the country and now were within a block of the railroad tracks. The rattle of the trains as they rumbled through the night left us all deprived of sleep that winter. First would come the long hoot of the whistle, and then the house would begin to shake. The walls would reverberate as the Great Northern train roared through town, tearing us from sleep and leaving us to toss and turn. When we finally had fallen asleep at last, it would roar through again at the edge of daylight. We never got used to it. In fact, we never got used to that town.

The first day of school I started out full of anticipation. I left early and got to school just as the busload of kids arrived. It wasn't what I expected. A tough little square-jawed girl with big spaces between her teeth challenged me before I could get across the schoolyard. When I tried to go past her, she jumped in front of me, and soon had a circle of kids around her. "Knock her down! Give her a bloody nose!" I was on the ground with my face being pushed in the dirt when I heard a man's voice, and the kids scattered. He yelled at them, but they were already out of sight. He told me he was the school principal and asked me my name. I was so humiliated that I could barely answer.

"You aren't hurt much," he said. "Come on, we'll get your face washed."

My stockings were torn and my knees were bloody. I had never been treated like that before in my life. If I went home, Maribelle would yell at me for getting dirty, so I thought might as well go on to school. I knew just how Mama felt. They couldn't bloody her face or tear her clothes, but they could damage her pride.

I don't remember much else about that little town. I get a sour taste in my mouth when I think about it, so it can't have been very good. I do remember going to church with Mama when she divided up her bridge winnings among us for the collection plate, and I kept mine to spend for candy.

Mama hadn't found a job for the following summer, and we couldn't pay the rent. There were a lot of people in circumstances like ours in those Depression days, but it was humiliating, and none of us ever forgot it. Flat broke, we went to visit our Uncle Hugh who lived on the east shore of Flathead Lake on the other side of the Rockies, two hundred miles away. Hugh and his wife were barely eking out a living, selling fruit and vegetables from their garden, and we didn't plan to stay long. Mama had applied to teach a summer school session in Kovich, south of Lewistown, and we all had high hopes.

We kids slept in tents outside, and even when it rained we enjoyed the adventure. I saw an oriole's nest hanging from a tree branch on one of our walks, and it was so delicate and beautiful I've never forgotten it. The beauty of the trees and mountains, and especially the lake, fascinated me. I had never seen so much water in one place. We walked to the lake every evening and ventured only into the shallowest part, as none of us dry land kids could swim. We all picked berries and helped with the weeding, and Mama made her marvelous pies for the roadside stand. They sold as fast as she could make them. I loved that place. It was so different from any place we had been, all leafy and green. But our aunt was sickly, and when the letter came with the new school contract we were relieved, but probably not as much as the relatives.

Summer School

Some of my memories of the new school south of Lewistown are clear as an April sky, and some are hazy. I know that it was a lovely setting, with green grass all around and lots of trees. There were ice caves and crystal caverns to be explored. Billy and I walked every daylight hour that we could get away.

Once when Mama and the girls came with us, we saw a small valley that seemed to reflect the orange lights of the sunset. When we drew closer we could see that it was carpeted with tiger lilies. They were a beautiful salmon color, sprinkled with black dots, and swaying on long slender stems. It was one of those rare moments that stand out in the greatest clarity. When I've told people about this, they tell me that tiger lilies don't grow wild. Maybe it was just the magic of that place, for that was the way the whole summer seemed to me—a sort of fairyland.

The school that Mama taught was attended and supported by a half-dozen or more Croatian families who still kept the old country ways. I was approaching thirteen that summer and was allowed to go along when some of the younger folks went to the dances. I got to dance a lot, which suited me just fine. I liked the Croatian way of doing things. Everyone danced, from the grandparents to the small children. Not a week went by that something wasn't going on, usually at the homes of one or the other of the families. They had kegs of home brew, with tin cups hanging on hooks around the edges. I was surprised when someone brought me a cup, but all the children over the age of ten drank beer right along with their elders. I knew Mama wouldn't approve, but I drank mine anyway. I didn't really like it much, but I drank more than I should have, because I woke up with a headache the next morning.

The women prepared great mounds of food and sat around gossiping and drinking beer, but they danced even if they had to dance with each other or one of the children. When they weren't dancing the men played a kind of bowling game in the yard. They called it "Croatia." There was a lot of laughing and friendly scuffling, and every so often one of the men would start to sing in a language I didn't recognize, and soon others would join him. The "old country" music from an accordion and guitar was hard to resist, and we danced until after midnight.

It was after one of these parties that I came home to find Mama crying. When I asked her what was wrong, she just turned her head and said, "Women have to cry about nothing sometimes. Please, go away and let me cry." When I put my arms around her, a chill ran through me. I knew with a terrible certainty that she would not live to see old age, and I began to cry with her. These momentary flashes of knowledge had come to me at other times as I was growing up. They were mostly just little things, like finding something that someone had lost or knowing that a package was about to arrive in the mail, but once in a while they left me wary and unsettled.

I especially remember the cabin in the woods. On one of our tramps we came upon a clearing with a pretty little peeled log house. A handsome white-haired man was sitting in front of it carving beautiful figures on a sort of chest. Suddenly I felt a chill run down my back, although it was a hot day. I pulled at Billy's sleeve. "Let's go," I said. The man was very thin and his skin was white and waxy. I felt as though I could see his bones like an x-ray.

He asked us what we were doing there and all but told us to leave. I grabbed Billy's arm and said "Come on!" but he was curious. He kept asking about the carving and wanted to know what it was for. The man gave him a tigerish look. "You really want to know? Well, I'll tell you. It's my coffin. Now git!" Neither of us said a word on the way home, and we never came upon that place again, although we walked that forest the rest of the summer.

Billy and I hitchhiked to Lewistown now and then and told awful lies to the people who picked us up. We were orphans traveling across the United States. We were Indians, working our way back to our tribe in Arizona. We were running away from an Orphans Home where we had been woefully mistreated. Sometimes we got a job pulling weeds in someone's garden and had enough money for a movie and a hot dog.

That was a wonderful summer. Ordinarily Billy would have had a job, but nobody had money to pay him. Since we had gone to school in the winter, we didn't really have to go to summer school, but Mama gave us assignments every day or so. I think she just wanted to know where we were. She'd have been really worried if she had known what we were up to most of the time. I left Lewistown with misgivings. The summer had certainly been magic.

The Hi-Line

When I was fourteen Mama was hired to teach in Inverness, one of the little Hi-Line towns that were scattered along the railroad tracks. They were strung from Chester to Havre, each with a school, two grain elevators, two churches (one Lutheran and one Catholic), and two flourishing bars. Of course there was always the general store that carried everything from shoes to long johns, along with groceries and fresh meat.

The year 1932 had promise of a good crop. The wheat stood high and golden awaiting the combines, and everyone was joyful and optimistic. Mama was promised a bigger salary than she'd ever had before, and the school board was to provide us with a three-bedroom house. We needed furniture, though, and didn't have the cash to buy secondhand, so with a lot of encouragement from the salesman in Havre, Mama decided to buy new. "Nothing down, Madam, and only ten dollars a month."

We were all lighthearted the day we moved in. The furniture smelled new, and the walnut-finished table and chairs just fit the dining room. We polished it with bee's wax every weekend and kept the house shining. I had never seen Mama happier. Then came the day when the thunder boomed and echoed across the prairie. Wind shrieked around the corners, and it turned bitterly cold in minutes. There was a roar that made the old-timers think briefly of tornadoes, such as they had seen in Kansas and other states they had left behind. They knew in their hearts what it was though, and the hail swept through, leaving devastation in its wake. A few vehicles headed out to assess the damage, but most of the farmers knew that the storm had been too intense to have left any grain standing.

Before long trucks and pickups were gathered around the Main Street bar. The farmers, whether to drown their sorrows or just to talk and plan for the next year, were there, shoulder to shoulder. There was a funereal atmosphere for a while. Everyone was hurt. Grocery bills that had been carried on the books all summer were left unpaid. New trucks were repossessed. Plans for a new tractor, washing machine, sofa, all had to be put aside now. We kids felt sorry for the farmers, not realizing what an impact it had on our own future, but little by little it became apparent that the troubles of the community were our troubles as well. The biggest shock was when Mama went to the store to cash her warrant.

"I've been informed by the school board that there may not be enough money in the school funds to cover the teachers' warrants," Mr. Warren said.

"But . . . what are we to do?" Mama looked stunned.

"I'll cash it, but since I'm taking a gamble, I'll have to take a percentage off the top," he said. "I'm sorry."

There was nothing left to do. She had to pay the utilities and the coal bill, so she turned the warrant over—with the discount. The next day she wrote a letter to the manager of the furniture store telling him that she could no longer make the payments. He was not surprised. It had happened before. When the farmers were hurting, everyone was hurting. Knowing that these things were happening to others didn't reduce the sting when the truck came to carry it all away. I was humiliated as only a self-centered teen can be, but the look in Mama's eyes was what hurt the most. I don't think she'd ever had anything new in her life, and it stung to lose it all so soon. She never complained, but instead pointed out how much worse it was for the farmers. And so, as we always did, we made the best of it.

Having lived in the country, isolated from other families all our lives, high school, with Latin and algebra and its social system, was difficult for all of us, Mama included, but we had some good teachers who made school fun. We were encouraged to play in the band, although we hadn't had any musical training at all. Earl Holden was the music instructor, and the first week he handed me a clarinet and Billy a piccolo. "I'm going to teach you how to play some real music," he said. "By next spring you'll be marching down Main Street in Havre tooteling with the best of them."

Mr. Holden was about five foot four and had curly blonde hair that seemed to stand on end when we hit sour notes. He appeared much taller when he snapped his baton in two and stomped off the stage, which he did regularly. We lost track of how many batons he ruined before spring. We started music lessons that first week of school, and he soon had us playing a march that still rings in my ears. We played it over and over twice a week from September to May, the same tune, until I could hear it in my dreams. Everyone in school who could carry an instrument played in the band. The fact that very few kids in the school could read music didn't faze him a bit.

Our English teacher, Miss Rollins, was a dainty little doll with honey blond hair and big brown eyes. She had a surprisingly strong soprano voice for one so small. Every girl in her English class adored her, and we even formed a secret Miss Rollins club.

The crowning event of the year for me was being chosen as one of the chorus girls for the school carnival. We were to wear black silk stockings and black satin shorts, high heels, and top hats. Miss Rollins held a leg contest with Mr. Holden as judge, and he chose me first of all. When I danced across the stage I felt pretty for the first time in my life. I think they knew how much it meant to me, the awkward new kid from the country.

In January Mr. Holden announced tryouts for the "Hallelujah Chorus," which he planned to direct. Singers came from all the Hi-line towns from Joplin to Kremlin. Mama, Billy, Donna, and I were among those chosen, and the practice sessions were something we looked forward to each week.

It was plain to see that a romance was blossoming between Miss Rollins and Mr. Holden. Once during practice she fainted dead away, and he dismissed the practice and carried her to his car. A week later some of us girls heard her throwing up in the bathroom, and gossip began to fly. Shortly after that she began wearing smocks to school. We called a meeting of the club, and the next day several of us girls wore smocks, too. When school started again after Easter, Miss Rollins went to the blackboard and wrote Mrs. Earl Holden. "That's my name now, class," she said. We were wildly excited, and planned a bridal shower for her. A few weeks later we had a baby shower.

We continued to labor away at that dreadful march, and the day of the music festival in Havre dawned bright and sunny and stayed that way, getting hotter by the minute as we trudged all the way from the fairgrounds to the college, never missing a note. Even the top of my head was sunburned, along with every inch of exposed skin. Mr. Holden pranced along in his blue satin suit and white-feathered hat, leading the band every painful step of the way. Thoughts of the street dance that night kept me going, but by the time the parade was over our feet were so blistered we could hardly walk. My friends and I opted for a movie instead.

The Holdens left Inverness the day after school was dismissed for the summer and weren't hired back. We girls cried and tried to console each other, and we managed to go on with our lives in spite of our sorrow.

I had just entered the "terrible teens," and I was as mean as spit. Finger waves were all the rage, and I had discovered a talent for it. My Saturdays were full, going from house to house "doing" hair at twenty-five cents a head all day long. On Friday night I would boil up a cup of flaxseed and water, let it set over night and strain it, making an oozy brown gunk that was guaranteed to turn a head of hair into a tin helmet.

Mrs. Qualley, the wife of the chairman of the school board, insisted that I come to her place first, but when I arrived she wouldn't have her hair washed. There was always a pile of ironing or a load of dishes waiting in the sink, and "couldn't I just touch up a few things while she washed her hair?" She needed a lesson.

There was going to be a dance the next Saturday night, and I had met a kid at the last ball game who was going to be there. My sister had a pair of silk stockings that I coveted and meant to have as my own if I could just figure out a way to get them from her. I imagined myself dancing the night away, my award-winning legs flashing in Maribelle's silken hose, and I came up with a diabolical plan.

The morning of the dance I smiled my most winning smile as I offered to "do" Mama's hair first, and then Maribelle's, so they would have all day to dry.

"But won't Mrs. Qualley be upset if you keep her waiting?" Mama said.

"Well, she's kept me waiting enough times," I told her. "She can wait this time."

I finished Mama's hair and then sat Maribelle down, squishing a liberal glob of the goop into her hair. I waved one side of her head and turned her to face the mirror. "Do you like this hair-do?" I asked.

"Of course not," she said. "Not with only one side done!"

"I'll wave the other side if you let me wear your silk stockings tonight." I smiled at her reflection in the mirror.

She was shocked that I would even dare to suggest something so outrageous. I had to be joking. "Come on, now," she said. "Quit fooling around and finish fixing my hair."

I went to get my coat. "Mrs. Qualley will be waiting," I said, and I was almost sorry I had started the whole thing. Almost.

"Mama!" she screamed. "Make her finish my hair."

Nothing would budge me. When she gave me the stockings, I hid them in a good place, finished the hair-do and then went on to Mrs. Qualley's place. Mrs. Qualley was livid, but I soothed her ruffled feathers and she forgave me. She had to. There wasn't anyone else in town to do her hair.

I had a wonderful time at the dance. The kid I had met turned out to be a good dancer, and we danced almost every number. Maribelle was a different story. Although I saved my quarters and had the storekeeper send for a new pair of stockings just for her, and even though I did her chores for a month and ironed her clothes, she stayed mad.

The day finally arrived when I was asked out on a date. I don't remember now what he looked like, but I was thrilled beyond belief. I had nearly a week to finish sewing a dress I had started, and I fixed my hair in a different style every day before deciding just how I wanted it for my debut. I intended to dazzle him with my charm and beauty. On Friday night I went to bed early. The next day I only had to wash and set my hair to be ready for the big night. I went to sleep thoroughly pleased with myself.

When I lifted my head from the pillow the next morning half of my hair stayed there. It had been cut off just above my left ear. Maribelle!

My life was over. I would have to hide out for a month. I would have to run away from home. I felt like screaming and kicking the walls, but I knew that was just what my sister was waiting to hear. Instead, I dressed and sneaked out. The husband of one of my finger-wave customers was the town barber, and he did the best he could with it. His wife tried to soothe me. "You just go home and get out your curling iron, Honey, and you'll look like a little doll," she said.

Just like a little doll, I thought, wiping away my tears as I looked in the mirror. Then I went home and announced that I had decided to wear my hair short for a while. Maribelle laughed so hard she nearly choked. I pretended that nothing was wrong, which was just about the hardest thing I had ever done. That night, I spent an hour with the curling iron and managed a curly mop that was a far cry from what I had planned for this rite of passage. When my date came to pick me up that night, he stopped short. I could see he wanted to ask me what had happened to my hair, but he just swallowed a couple of times. "Well, let's go," he said.

I didn't offer any explanation, but although I enjoyed the dance, I knew he wouldn't ask me out again. He didn't. By the time my hair grew out I had saved enough quarters to have my first permanent and had another boyfriend.

High School

I was with a giggling bunch of schoolgirls when I first saw my future husband. We were living in Hingham, where Mama had gotten another teaching job. I had turned sixteen in October. We were seeing a friend off on the train who was on his way back to college after Christmas break, when I saw a man with the most beautiful shade of red hair that I had ever seen. When I was six years old I had fallen in love with a redheaded classmate and had sworn that when I got old enough I would marry a man with red hair. I wish I could say that this was he, that little redheaded boy of my childhood, grown up, but alas, not so. I caught the man looking at me and asked one of the girls who he was. "That's Pinky Sterry," she said, "but Margaretta Kersey has her eye on him, so don't get your hopes up."

I looked for him at every dance after that and was just about to give up when he walked in one Saturday night. When the ladies were just putting out the sandwiches for the supper, I felt a tap on my shoulder. There he was, and he was asking me for the supper dance. It happened that Margaretta and I were wearing dresses made from the same pattern. Hers was pink and mine was green, and I think to this day that he thought I was Margaretta when he tapped me on the shoulder. Years later, when I found out he was color-blind, I asked him, but he only grinned and gave me a hug. He asked me to go to the movies the next week, and I knew, even if he didn't, that I had found my redheaded man.

Looking to make up for all the years we lived in isolated schoolhouses, I was ready to enjoy being a girl. There were dances in one of the Hi-Line towns every weekend, and someone was always able to rustle up a car. We all chipped in with a quarter, or whatever we could spare, for gas.

Mama had been given a house, not quite as grand as the one in Inverness the year before, but it had three bedrooms upstairs and a coal cellar in the dugout basement. I remember that coal cellar with a lump in my throat. It was the source of embarrassment one cold winter day. Mama had ordered a load of coal, but the school board was late with the warrants. When we came home from school the men were just finishing unloading the last of it. I was sent to tell them to come back the next day for their pay. Obviously, they had been counting on that money for groceries or some other necessities. They didn't say a word, but just climbed down into the bin and started shoveling all the coal back into the truck. It was at times like these that we felt the pinch of Depression the most.

Hingham was a town of nicknames. Almost everybody had one. Alton's brother was called "Deacon," because he taught Sunday school one year. Alton's father Olaf was called "Whispering Ole." I think it was the salesman in him. He always lowered his voice when he was selling a "bargain." Of course, it could have been because of his frequent bouts of laryngitis. I don't know who the author was of all those names, but once you got a nickname, it stuck, and I never heard Alton called anything but "Pinky." He said he guessed that one of the teachers gave him that name because he blushed so easily.

One of the special things that set that little town apart from the others on the Hi-Line was that it was built around a park, and all the streets were laid out around it. A large sign, mounted on the highway, proudly proclaimed: "Hingham, the Town on the Square." When our family arrived in 1933, Hingham had a bandstand and boasted a band concert every week or so in the summer. The park was a good place for the little kids to play tag until they were called in at bedtime and a fine place for us older kids to sit and hold hands and maybe steal a kiss or two.

The Kersey Hotel, owned by our friend, Ida Kersey, was on the northwest corner. The weekly newspaper, the *Hi-Line Herald*, and the barbershop were next door. Diagonally across from the hotel was the red brick building that had once been the Hingham Bank, but was now the Bank Bar, one of three bars in this little town. It had a dark history. The bartender had been found dead, and the cash drawer empty, one chilly morning many Decembers earlier. The murderer was never found.

Next to the Bank Bar was the Odd Fellows Hall, where most of the town's entertainment was centered. There were dances every week or so, declamation contests, spelling bees, and twice a month a Havre couple brought us a movie. The folding chairs would be set up, the faded canvas curtain lowered, and the M.G.M. lion would roar across the screen. Alton and I had our first real date there and shyly held hands when the lights were turned off.

The only other building of any consequence besides the schoolhouse, which sat grandly next to the highway, was the Hingham Bar, its name spelled out in twinkling red and blue lights. This was where the farmers met to lie about their yield, complain about the lack of rain, the coldness of their wives, or the fickleness of the government. In later years this was also the core of many family arguments concerning husbands who sat warming the stools while their supper cooled at home. The phone would ring, the bartender would call out a name, "Bob . . . Charlie . . . Pinky," and then, "No, he just left fifteen minutes ago."

I was a sophomore in high school, and just as goofy as sixteen-year-old girls are today. I loved living in town, and I loved going to school even though the other girls were pretty hard on me at first. One thing I hated was gym class. It wasn't that I didn't like exercise, but I was a late bloomer and skinny at that. Those were the days of Jane Russell and the up-lift bra, and if you couldn't fill one, you just didn't "measure up." Having to take a shower with all those B and C cups was just too intimidating. So I skipped the showers and bought a set of rubber falsies like any self-respecting flat-chested girl. One day after gym class, when I had once again missed the shower, I walked into the assembly room to dead quiet.

I suspected then that some of the girls had set a trap for me. When I reached into my desk to get a book, a rubber falsie fell on the floor. And bounced! Amid smothered giggles my first reaction was to check to see if I still had what I'd left home with, but that would have been too obvious. I decided to brazen it out. I reached for it, but only managed to knock it out into the aisle, where it lay in plain sight. It was so pink it was almost pulsating when I picked it up and stuffed it back into my desk. By that time everyone, including the principal, was laughing. It was some time before the room quieted down, but I'd had my "initiation," and the other girls warmed up to me after that. I was glad I hadn't burst into tears.

We had a school principal the like of which I have never seen before or since. Mr. Swatek could reduce you to a simpleton with one of his piercing glances. It didn't do to try to be a smart-aleck with him. I know from personal experience. He had deep creases on each side of his face, starting at the corners of his eyes, and disappearing under his chin. This, along with his little pointed goatee, gave him the look of a clever gargoyle. I often wondered how he managed to shave.

He knew us all, our faults and virtues if such there were, and spent his spare time thinking up ways to foil our schemes. One Halloween he pulled one of his greatest coups. There was no indoor plumbing in Hingham at that time, and the ambition of every boy in the school was to push Mr. Swatek's outhouse over on Halloween. When the kids spilled out of the school bus, they saw that it had not only been pushed over, but had been roped and dragged clear up to his front step.

When we came giggling into the schoolhouse, Mr. Swatek watched as we took our seats, his face impassive, giving nothing away. At the noon hour he had a list of the names of nearly all the boys in high school written on the blackboard. When we were in our seats he strode to the front of the room and stood there with his arms crossed, staring at each of the culprits. The long silence was painful.

Then, one by one, he called each boy up in front of the room. "All right, you little shysters," he said. "Let me see the soles of your shoes." He had outwitted them again, first putting a layer of sawdust all around the toilet, and then by soaking it liberally with crankcase oil. There was no way out of it. Their oily tracks were everywhere. I don't remember just what their punishment was, but for starters, I know they had to dig a new "depository" for the outhouse and mount it again in all its glory.

One raw day in November 1934, Margie, my future sister-in-law, and I walked home for lunch hour. Margie, Alton's sister and I, were best friends, but we were as different as thumbprints. She was a good student, and I was a moth in search of a flame. It was my second year in Hingham. I had stayed behind when Mama took a job at a country school, and Margie and I were rooming together at a house about three-quarters of a mile from the school. I had to do a lot of coaxing to get her to go home with me. She didn't know that I wasn't going back to school after lunch and that I was planning to coerce her into playing hooky with me. Our landlady had gone to Havre for the day, so I knew she wouldn't be there to foil my plans.

I used all my powers of persuasion to get Margie to stay. I had just convinced her, and she was settled down with a book, when we looked out the window and saw Mr. Swatek heading down the lane, his scarf blowing in the wind. Margie turned white and hit for the stairs. "Don't tell him I'm here," she quavered.

I was just as scared as she was, but I decided to bluff it out, my brain working overtime to come up with an excuse for being home at 1:30 in the afternoon. I watched his approach with all the fascination of a rabbit in the path of a rattler about to strike, but when he hammered on the door, I was ready for him.

Opening it with a flourish, I said, "Come on in, Mr. Swatek. We were just about to come back to school. You see, Mrs. Almos asked us to come home and take her bread out of the oven."

He lifted his head and sniffed like a cat.

"I don't smell any bread," he said. Then going over to the stove, he opened the oven. It was cold and empty. Giving me a withering glance, he said, "Now you go upstairs and get Margie wherever she's hiding and bring her on down here. You two have a long afternoon in front of you. We're going back to school." It was an embarrassing walk back, and I can still hear his overshoes flapping as he marched us along in front of him.

We were not only humiliated in front of the whole assembly, but we had to stay after school and help the janitor wash the blackboards. Margie was furious, and her face was as red as her hair as we stood there taking our tongue-lashing. She never blamed me for getting her into that mess. As she said, nobody forced her to go along with me. I felt guilty, though, as she was an excellent scholar, and actually one of Mr. Swatek's favorites.

We always had a special program on the last Friday of the month. Once Mr. Swatek played the violin while Miss Mulliken, the English teacher, narrated the story of Peer Gynt. It made a big impression on me then, and as I grew older, I could imagine the hours of practice it had taken those dedicated teachers just to educate and entertain us. Mr. Swatek, a self-professed expert on baseball, even brought a radio to study hall and let us listen to the World Series one October. I'm not sure that all this was entirely for our edification only, but it was a good idea as far as I was concerned. I learned to love the game, and Alton and I never missed a World Series in all the years we had together.

One Friday the teachers put on a skit that had the whole school laughing. I don't remember just what it was Mr. Swatek said, but it made Margie the butt of a joke. That time she was mad clear through. I could tell by the white line around her mouth that she wasn't going to take this lying down. That afternoon when we were gathering up our things to go home, she said, "Wait here for me, I have a little business to attend to." Of course I followed and was right behind her when she rapped on the door of Mr. Swatek's office.

He jumped up, all smiles. "What can I do for you, Margie?" he asked.

"You can go to hell, Mr. Swatek," she said and slammed the door on her way out.

We could hear him laughing all the way down the hall, which only added to Margie's fury. If it had been anyone else, he would have made life unbearable for months, but I think he knew that he had overstepped his bounds this time.

Miss Mulliken, the English teacher, could scorch you with a glance. She had a sharp tongue and a wit to match. Very few of us got away with anything in her class, but some of the boys drove her to distraction. I must admit that I wasn't a favorite of many teachers, but she favored me because I actually liked Shakespeare. She had an unfortunate figure, with big bony hips and practically no bosom at all, and she often lectured us on the virtues of chastity. "Just think how stupid it would be to ruin your future for a few seconds of ecstasy," she said one day.

I thought I must have heard her wrong.

"A few seconds?" I thought. Was that the big deal the boys and some of the girls snickered about behind their hands in the hallways? I don't know how the mothers of this generation would have reacted, but we got lectures on social behavior and sex education sprinkled among the Shakespeare sonnets on a daily basis.

I think she relished confrontations with her students, and the boys, my brother in particular, gave her plenty of those. We had lived among books all our lives, and when there wasn't anything else to read, we read, and enjoyed, Shakespeare. One time, she called on my brother to recite a portion of *Romeo and Juliet*, and he started reciting, but with a book held in front of his face. "I didn't say read it, Billy, I said recite it," she said, jerking the book away from him. He never faltered, but just kept on "reading" the lines without the book and turning invisible pages, while Miss Milliken stood there steaming.

One day she had suffered enough, and she took Billy out in the hallway. "I'll make a deal with you," she said. "I know you are well versed in what I'm teaching here, but you're making it hard for me to teach the others. I'll give you an A if you'll just stay the hell out of my classroom. Oh yes, and I expect you to have a long piece memorized for declamation next month."

Billy was working for a farmer after school and on weekends and forgot his end of the bargain. Just in time he remembered "The Face on the Bar-Room Floor" that he had memorized when he was a kid. Although he didn't get first place in the declamation contest, all of the judges except one gave him top marks. The one dissenter was the wife of our local minister. He received his "A" in English, however, and found he liked declamation so much that he went on and took first place in the state his junior year. It happened that just before the class was to leave for the state meet in Helena, the crank on the tractor hit him in the face, breaking off one of his front teeth. Billy went to the meet anyway and won. When he was waiting in line to go up and receive his award, he heard someone ask who won first in the humorous division?

"Oh, some big ugly galoot with his tooth out in front," was the reply.

Young Love

In 1934 I was sixteen, living in Hingham where I was a junior in high school. Mama was teaching at a country school, just a few miles from the school at which Alton, then twenty-one, was teaching. Every other Friday night Alton took me to a movie in Hingham, but that weekend we were headed for a dance at Goldstone. It was an inland town about ten miles from the Canadian border with a post office and a store that supplied the community with necessities like kerosene, coal, and the most basic of groceries. It wasn't much of a store, but for some reason Goldstone always seemed to have the best dances. Excitement filled the air as the floor was slicked with cornmeal and the musicians tuned their instruments.

It was an unspoken rule that although you might arrive as a couple the girls always gathered on one side of the hall and the boys on the other. After the first number it was every man for himself. Some of the girls filled their dance card as many as three or four dances ahead, but Alton always claimed every other dance, so I was never the social butterfly I longed to be. A pair of Sears Roebuck's best $3.95 shoes didn't last long on those Hi-Line dance floors, but my finger-wave money kept me dancing.

The dance band was made up of local fellows, and Mel Kinchey, the trombonist, was from Hingham. He was a menace to any couple foolhardy enough to dance too close to the stage. His trombone would swoop out and catch the hem of the girls' skirts and lift them embarrassingly high. This was usually good for a laugh the first time he did it, but as it got later, Mel would go too far, and somebody's boyfriend would threaten to knock his block off if he didn't cut it out.

This dance was an event I had been looking forward to, and I was miserable. My head ached and I felt like my face was on fire, but I wouldn't let Alton take me home until the last dance was over. The next morning my face was covered with red blotches. I had chicken pox.

When Alton came knocking on the door the next night I refused to let him in. I had big pocks on my face and forehead and my eyes were red and swollen.

"But, Honey," he said. "You don't have to worry about me, I already had chicken pox."

Men!

Mama argued on his side the next night, and I grudgingly let him in, but I plastered make-up over the pocks and have scars today to prove it.

That summer Alton went back to Northern Montana College in Havre to renew his teaching certificate, and Mama and us kids moved to Havre, too. Mama got a job making pies in Buttreys' coffee shop, and it became a popular place for those who could afford it. The price of a piece of pie and a cup of coffee was thirty-five cents. You could buy a hot beef sandwich with mashed potatoes and gravy for a dollar.

After we moved to Havre I got a series of little jobs—walking dogs, helping with housework, ironing clothes, anything for a little cash. When Alton and I weren't totally broke, we rented a bicycle for two and bought a bag of popcorn. I think it cost us fifteen cents. Alton had to write down every nickel and what he spent it for and give the list to Ole at the end of the month, so we didn't spend much. When it was time to return the bike we would sit on the back steps and neck until Mama came out and turned on the light. I thought it was terribly romantic.

I found a job cooking for an old bachelor during harvest, but I wouldn't go unless my sister Bette went along. His name was Victor Kawalsky, and he seemed like a nice old guy. He had a good reputation in Kremlin, so Mama felt confident that we would be safe there. I didn't know much about cooking, but we did the best we could to put decent food on the table. We also washed and ironed the curtains, scrubbed the floor, and even washed and mended his work clothes. There was an old horse that we could ride bareback when the work was done, and we were beginning to enjoy ourselves. Then, suddenly, the grain was ripe and he hired a man to help with the harvest. I'm sure he was a transient from the railroad yards.

"This here's Sonny," he told us.

Sonny always seemed to stand a little too close, and every time we looked up, his watery eyes would be staring at us, especially my thirteen-year-old sister, Bette. He wore tan coveralls and seemed to be the same color from the top of his sandy hair, eyebrows, and moustache to his feet. Even his eyes looked yellow. They barely got three days of harvesting done when we had an afternoon rain. That night the two men went to town, and when they returned Sonny was drunk. They appeared to be settled down, or at least we didn't hear anyone walking around, but we moved the heavy dresser up against the door before we went to bed. I was just beginning to relax, and Bette was asleep, when I heard scratching and whispering at the door.

"Hey! Hey! Let's have a little party."

Bette was awake now, too, and we were terrified, but decided that anything was better than staying there, so we gathered our blankets and crawled out the window, heading for the barn. We were afraid every minute that Sonny would come outside and catch us before we could climb on the horse and get away, but we made it to the gate and down the hill to the pasture. There was a thin fingernail of a moon that night. Although it was August we spent an uncomfortable night huddled beneath our blankets and were shivering before morning. I didn't sleep at all, and Bette slept only in snatches. Buffaloberry bushes grew along the low spots, loaded with fruit, bright red in the milky moonlight, and I remember their tart pungent taste and the stomachache I had the next day.

Sunrise never looked so good. When we told our boss that morning about his hired man's attempt to get into our room, he just laughed and said we were imagining things. When I told him it was either us or the hired man, he didn't take long to think about it. He just told me to get our things. He didn't take us home until after he got another cook, though, and I didn't think the hired man would bother her any. She must have weighed three hundred pounds, and she had a face like a map of the Montana badlands.

I started working nights at a restaurant after that and didn't have so much time on my hands. I was testing my wings a little and began going out with other fellows. I guess Alton had other girlfriends, too, but after an on-again, off-again romance we were married in 1937. I wanted a church wedding with all my friends there, but Alton just wanted to go to a J.P., so we compromised. I took Mama to lunch and told her of our plans. She was happy for me, and I knew she would have liked to be there with us, but she couldn't leave her job. So Alton and I went to Great Falls, and with Maribelle and her current boyfriend as attendants, promised to love and honor each other as long as we both should live. We were married in a lovely little Lutheran church, and I felt as truly married as a white-gowned bride with a half-dozen bridesmaids. Alton had reserved the bridal suite at the Johnson Hotel. It was elegant, with a sunken tub, and he even had a bottle of champagne on ice. I couldn't have felt more cherished.

Immediately after the wedding, right after we left the church, my new husband spoke to me solemnly. "I have just one request. From now on, call me Alton. I've always hated being called Pinky."

Our first summer together Alton got a job working on the spillway of Fresno Dam west of Havre, and I enjoyed playing house and feeling all grown up. He didn't want to go back to the drudgery of the farm and was happy in his work. One day he managed to ignite a bunch of farmer matches in his pocket and had a serious burn on his thigh as big as a man's hand. I dressed the burn daily, but it became infected by concrete dust, and he had to quit his job. It was back to the farm for us, and Ole was only too happy to have him there for the rest of the summer. I spent my time hoeing the long rows of corn and generally learning from Maggie how to be a farm wife. I didn't think anyone could make piecrust as well as my mother, but Maggie could, so I practiced until I got it right.

Alton's school that year was south of Rudyard, and the old-timers would talk about the winter of '38 for years to come. There were snowdrifts as high as the roof of the schoolhouse on one side, and it was bitterly cold. We always made it back to the farm on weekends, though, with Alton shoveling through the drifts. One of the car windows was cracked, and we put a piece of cardboard over it. I remember breathing that cold air as it almost sealed our nostrils with every breath. We heated rocks in the oven and put them at our feet, I would button my coat over my bulging stomach, and off we'd go. How wonderful it was to relax in the warmth of Maggie's kitchen and enjoy her cooking. Sometimes Olaf would get out his fiddle and play some of the old tunes he had played as a young man at the dances. Maggie would sit and tap out the steps and imagine, perhaps, that she was once again a light-footed, popular girl. That was the beginning of nearly sixty years that Alton and I had together.

Homesteaders

Alton's parents, along with other Montana homesteaders, had been promised so much, and dry land farming proved more of a gamble than they could have imagined. When they first arrived in Hingham, they settled in the old Hingham Hotel until they could find and file on a homestead. The hotel was a two-story structure with tarpaper siding and no divisions for rooms. Wire was stretched from wall to wall with blankets pinned up marking each family's cubicle in which they kept their belongings until their shack was built. Once I asked Olaf why they ever left an established business—a small country store in North Dakota—to travel to that hard-scrabble place. "We were young and we owed money to the bank and the land was free," he said. "Is that reason enough for you?"

I could never get Alton's mother to tell about the early days, but Olaf was a talker. The hardest part, he said, was finding a horse and buggy to go out and look for their claim. He told of horses literally being driven to death, for it was hard to judge the distance in that flat and treeless plain.

They came from strong stock, those hardy Bohemians and Norwegians who settled the country and raised families, who started the churches and built the schools. They broke and plowed and planted the land, and at first the crops were bountiful, the tall wheat blowing sweetly in the wind. The brochures sent out by the railroads to lure people to Montana promised sixteen inches of rain every year. How could they lose?

Then came the seasons of drought, and they watched the fields turn brown in mid-summer. Then again they were blessed with rain only to see the hail destroy in minutes what had taken a year of drudgery to grow. And then the grasshoppers flew in, clouds of them, leaving only ragged stubble in their wake. Would-be farmers sold their 320 acres for what they could get and returned east in defeat. Some simply turned their stock loose and moved on west.

Olaf and Maggie were among those who stayed, but he wasn't really a farmer at heart. Generations of Sterrys had been storekeepers. Selling was one thing Olaf knew he could do. With Maggie's help he got one more crop in and it flourished. He contacted the McNess Company and became their representative, selling liniment and vanilla and everything in between. He bought a horse and buggy, and his territory took him north to the Canadian border, twenty-five miles away, and to Fort Benton, fifty miles in the other direction. In this way he kept his family in necessities and seed wheat when the crops failed while other farmers in the area gave up one by one.

Olaf could play anything on the fiddle, and he was a welcome guest at the stark and joyless households throughout the long stretches of prairie. He could count on being invited to stay for supper and given hay and shelter for his horse and a bed for the night. I'm sure the farm families he visited thought it was a small price to pay for an evening of stories and toe-tapping music.

Maggie was a true pioneer woman. She had traveled with her mother, father, four sisters, and five brothers from Norway in 1884 when she was only twelve, settled in Iowa, and then moved on to Kansas where she and her girlfriends cooked for threshing crews. Her mother lived only a short time after coming to America. Some said it was homesickness for her green and mountainous homeland.

Maggie, on the other hand, thrived. She remained fiercely proud of her family, and never lost the dignity that came from knowing who she was and where she came from. She loved square dancing, and her five handsome brothers saw to it that she never sat out a dance and warned her of the fellows who were drinking. She was a good dancer, and until the day she died she would sit and follow all the dance steps to the music of Lawrence Welk from her straight-backed kitchen chair.

She met Olaf at one of those dances where he played the fiddle and flirted with the prettiest girls. She nearly drove him wild, pretending not to notice him as she danced by with other fellows. He finally got her attention when he laid down his fiddle and asked her to be his partner in the next square. After that he became her escort for nearly a year before he began cautiously to talk about marriage. Maggie kept him waiting for as long as she dared before agreeing to marry him and move to North Dakota, where Olaf ran a small country store and post office. They stayed there for five years until reports of free land enticed them west.

Two babies succumbed to the fierce North Dakota winters. What they thought were only simple colds turned out to be pneumonia. Maggie would never talk about the loss of her babies, or about how hard it had been to move on and leave their graves behind. She had another child in North Dakota and four more in Montana.

Alton was the first child born in Montana. At the time of his birth, Maggie had everything in readiness: sterilized string and scissors, lots of hot water, and a birthing pad. When she told Ole it was time to fetch the neighbor woman who lived a mile away, Ole galloped out of the yard and down the road. He must have gotten into a conversation, however, probably about politics since it was October and close to election time, and he didn't return with the neighbor woman for more than an hour. The baby couldn't wait, so she delivered Alton herself with the help of his three-year-old brother, Norman. Maggie was back in a clean bed, nursing her new little redhead when Ole returned with the neighbor, contrite at being late but proud of his new son.

All the water for the family's use had to be pumped by hand and hauled up the hill on a "stone boat," so called because it was used mainly for picking the relentless rocks that rose to the surface in the fields every spring. The stone boat was about twice the size of a barn door. It was flat, with poles attached to the bottom like runners on a sleigh. You had to ride in it standing up, and it was hard just keeping your balance as it was dragged over gravel and rocks. It was used to haul the winter's supply of coal from the Goldstone mines, a day's walk from the farm.

I often heard the story of the time nine-year-old Alton and twelve-year-old Norman left before daylight for those mines and didn't get home with the load of coal until after dark, their hands and feet aching with the cold and their stomachs aching from hunger. Their father was in Rochester, New York, where he had gone for surgery. He had developed kidney trouble and had to have a kidney removed. The family was grateful he survived and thankful when he finally recovered. During his convalescence, Maggie handled most of the farm work, with the help of the older children, all while nursing Ole back to health and taking care of two small children.

Ole and Maggie were a study in contrast. Ole was an outgoing, talkative man. He had a good strong tenor voice and often embarrassed his family by singing too loudly in church. A spitfire of a man, he was unkindly described by a town wag as a fart in a frying pan. I thought it was a good description. He and I never got along. Maggie, on the other hand, was a very quiet woman. Her family, the Amdahls, believed in letting others do the talking while they listened—and judged.

Throughout her marriage Maggie milked the cow, helped with the haying, harnessed and fed the horses, shoveled grain, and carried water to wash clothes by hand. There wasn't much she couldn't do, but there was one thing she wouldn't do: cut the head off a chicken. One time the threshing crew came before they were expected, and she didn't have any meat to fix for supper. She had to figure out a way to behead a couple of chickens without looking in their eyes. They were her pets, her friends, and she couldn't bear to see them die. She put their heads under the washtub, and then with one foot holding the tub down, she aimed, closed her eyes, and wielded the hatchet. The crew said they had never eaten better chicken, but Maggie couldn't eat a bite.

Olaf and Maggie were still living in the homestead shack when Alton and I were married in 1937. They managed to send three of their children to college by going without the comforts we take for granted today. Though Ole and I clashed frequently, I knew he was good man who meant to give his children the education he never had. One of the first families to settle in Hingham, the Sterrys were charter members of the Lutheran church and supported it financially through good times and bad. Their five children and five grandchildren were all baptized at that altar. Today Olaf and Maggie lie side by side in the Hingham cemetery on top of the hill, joined now by their son, my lifelong companion.

Mama, age eighteen

Mama, Irene, and Maribelle, 1914

Left to right: Uncle Fred, Aunt Ella, Mama, and Papa before Mama and Papa left the homestead

One of the many one-room prairie schools at which Mama taught

Haying at Big Sandy, circa 1922

Whitewater School, circa 1924. I am standing just left of Mama.

Nedra, eight, and Mirabelle, twelve, in front of Gildford School

Nedra, ten, and Billy, twelve

*From left to right, front row: Mama, Nedra, Bette, and Donna with Melvin
Tew (back right) and neighbors on Tew's ranch circa 1930*

*Nedra, right, age twelve, wearing
the first dress she sewed herself,
with her cousin, Agnes, at
Flathead Lake*

*Maribelle, Mama, Bette, and Nedra,
circa 1940*

Maggie *Olaf*

Alton, far right, 1938, with his students

Winter on the farm. Alton spent his early years in the homestead shack on the left.

Ricky, Craig, Alan, and Sandra, circa 1951, in front of the new car

Nedra and Craig, 1943

Sandra, circa 1948

Nedra and Ricky, age four, in front of the Capitol, Washington, D.C.

Craig, Sandra, Alan, and Rick, circa 1962

Alton and Nedra on their twenty-fifth wedding anniversary holding baby Jill

Wedded Bliss

My life didn't change all that much with marriage. In many ways, it was just another schoolhouse, another prairie, another one-room teacherage with snow blowing in around the doors and windows. The winter of 1937-38, as my belly grew, we had to work hard to avoid bumping into each other in the little space between the bed, table, and stove.

I still have a letter I began to write to my sister as I waited between contractions to give birth to our oldest child. "Dear Maribelle," I wrote: "How I wish you could be here with me today. I feel like a big baby. All I can do is cry. Alton can't be with me, either. Nobody ever told me it was going to hurt this much. There is a young woman across the hall who is having her first baby, and she screams and screams. I hear later that her baby is turned sideways, and the doctor has to turn it. Her name is Mrs. Musgrove, and she is from Chinook." The letter is streaked with tears as the words trail off across the page. I never did finish it. I was feeling pretty sorry for myself, not knowing how much worse it would be.

The doctor had decided on induced labor because I had high blood pressure, and I had been staying in Havre with my mother, so Alton couldn't be there during Ricky's birth. He came in the next morning, though, and after admiring his new son, asked me if there was anything he could get me from downtown. I didn't even have to think about it. Now that I could see my legs again, I wanted a pair of sheer, black silk stockings.

When he came bringing not only the stockings and a big box of chocolates, but a bouquet of flowers, I felt like a queen. I lay there with my legs encased in black silk, wearing a faded, scratchy hospital gown as we shared the chocolates and admired my legs. That was to be a tradition. No matter how busy he was or how broke we were, Alton brought me a box of chocolates when a new baby was born.

We named the baby Richard Arden. Alton's middle name was Richard, and Arden was my name spelled backwards. We thought we were awfully clever to choose a name that made him our special child. And he was special. I didn't realize it then, but he was an exceptionally good baby. He seldom cried, and he smiled early, which delighted the grandmas and aunts.

We brought Ricky home from the hospital in our old Model A on a blustery winter day. It stayed cold that winter, and the only way we could be sure the baby was warm enough was to take him into bed with us. He was a tough little kid, surviving his young mother's mistakes and flourishing on whatever we fed him. Grandma gave him his first taste of solid food—mashed potatoes and gravy—and we started him on cream of wheat when he was two months old. We went home to the farm every weekend, and it was wonderful. I wasn't much of a cook, and Maggie would always have crusty fresh bread stacked on the table and a beef roast or fried chicken in the oven.

Alton got a teaching job the next winter north of Hingham, and we had to stretch his eighty-dollar paycheck to make payments to the hospital for Ricky's birth. I was there for a whole week, and I think the entire bill was sixty-five dollars. They used to keep us in the hospital that long and wouldn't even let us get out of bed. By the time I got home my legs were like rubber from lack of exercise.

There was a reservoir near the school, and though neither of us knew how to skate we sent away for skates for both of us. We had to do a lot of figuring on the back of an envelope to justify such an expenditure. The skates cost $3.95 a pair. We had a lot of spills, but nothing serious, and we did learn to skate. We bought a secondhand sled for Ricky, and we would take turns pulling him across the ice.

When it warmed up in the spring Ricky played outside for hours. I found out one sunny day just what he was up to. He was raiding the school kids' lunch boxes! One day he got a little reckless, and I caught him with the goods. He had all the lunch boxes lined up in a row as he browsed among them. Surely the kids must have missed their goodies, but nobody had said a word.

Alton left teaching the following year. It was 1941, and the threat of war hung over all our heads. Knowing that there would be a shortage of trained workers if the United States entered the conflict raging in Europe, the Civil Service Administration sent out brochures encouraging people like Alton to take the exams. Alton really wanted to go back to college and teach, but knew he couldn't with a wife and child to support, so he filled out an application. He studied far into the night by the light of the kerosene lamp. Ricky and I were always asleep by the time he came to bed, but his hard work paid off. Sooner than we expected he received a letter with a contract. He was to have a job with the Federal Printing Office in Washington, D.C., and they wanted him as soon as he could get away. He would leave right after the school term ended, and I was already beginning to feel lonesome.

We had been squeezing nickels, trying to get enough money together for his train fare and to live on until his first paycheck, but we couldn't quite make it. We had to borrow the money from Ole, and Alton hated having to ask. Ole didn't want Alton to leave the farm, so he made it as tough as possible, and any secret hopes I had of Ricky and me going to D.C. with Alton were nipped in the bud. Alton's folks could only wait and hope that he would get so lonely without us that he'd come back and run the farm.

I hated living on the farm without Alton. Ole and I argued frequently, and he knew just how to put his needles in where they hurt. What enraged me most was when he and Maggie started speaking Norwegian to each other. It didn't take much for me to feel like an outsider, and that really made me feel shut out. I couldn't have been a very pleasant person to have around, either. By July I'd had enough, and went to see Maggie's sister-in-law Ella. She didn't get along with Ole, either, and I think she gave me the money for train fare just to spite him. I felt sorry for

Maggie, though, having her only grandchild taken so far away, and I promised to write often. My mother felt just as bereft, I'm sure, but they both put a brave face on it.

I was excited and full of enthusiasm when we boarded the train that hot summer day. Ricky was fretful and flushed and didn't want to leave his grandma's arms. She had never shown her feelings before, but I saw her wipe away a tear as the train began to leave the station. My mother was crying openly, but it touched me less because it was what I expected. I hated to leave her, too.

I can't remember much about that long train ride. Ricky hadn't slept well the night before, and I took him into the Chicago station where he could run around, and then into the women's rest room where there was a crib to put him in. He went right to sleep, and I sat there on the floor until it was time to board the train. I was beginning to find out that traveling with a small child wasn't easy.

We only had one double seat, and I fixed him a bed on it so he could stretch out, and he was soon asleep. There was an empty seat across the aisle, and the little man who occupied the other seat looked harmless. He had a thin patch of hair plastered across a freckled bald spot and straggly white eyebrows. I studied him for a while, decided he wasn't a threat, and then asked if I could use the other seat.

He didn't say anything, but patted the seat beside him. Just as I was dozing off, he laid his hand on my thigh and started whispering. "I'll bet you miss your husband, honey. How long has he been gone?"

I was shocked and angry, but I didn't know what to do. I jumped up and was still standing in the aisle when the conductor came along and asked me what the trouble was. My erstwhile seat partner pretended to be asleep, but the conductor guessed what the situation was. "Has this guy been bothering you, little lady?" He asked. He tapped him on the shoulder. "Come along with me, fellow. I have a seat partner down in the next car that's just right for you. She outweighs you by at least a hundred pounds." The little weasel gave me a dirty look as he followed the conductor down the aisle.

When the train rolled into Union Station and I saw Alton standing there waiting for us, it was worth it all: the long wait on the farm, Ole's orneriness, and leaving my own mother. I wonder if I would have gone if I had known that I would never see Mama again.

City Kids

Housing was hard to find that summer in Washington, D.C., but Alton met two young men who were going to be his coworkers, and they helped him secure an apartment in their building just across the line in Mt. Rainier, Maryland. He bought a mattress and spring on time, and even though the place looked bare, I thought it was wonderful. Everything looked so new and shiny. The wooden floors were all newly varnished, and when you opened a pair of double doors, there was a tiny kitchen.

I was less enthusiastic when I got up in the middle of the night for a drink of water to find the kitchen literally swarming with bugs such as I had never seen before. Alton was working the graveyard shift, so Ricky and I were alone, and I didn't sleep any more that night. Even though this was a brand new building we were to carry on a never-ending battle with the cockroaches, and I never got used to them.

When we were able to pay off our debts we went looking for some furniture. There were ads in all the papers: "Two rooms of furniture with no down payment," and although Alton was reluctant to get into debt, I coaxed until he gave in. We got a table and chairs, a bed and a davenport that converted into a bed for Ricky, all for $95.99—and only $10.00 a month.

It was an exciting time, and I loved everything about the city and our new life. We were thrilled at being in the nation's capital, and we made good use of our free time. We would pack a lunch and take Ricky with us to see the Lincoln Memorial one weekend and the Washington Monument another. We took pictures every place we went. We were not allowed into the White House during those troubled times, but went to the Capitol and all the other important buildings often. When the guards insisted upon looking through my handbag I was embarrassed at having personal items in there. It didn't take much to embarrass me in those days.

Once we were lucky enough to be in the Capitol when Montana senator Burton K. Wheeler was there, and the three of us were invited to ride the underground trolley over to the Senate building with him. We were proud when he took Ricky's hand and showed him around the room, and even Ole was impressed when we told him about that.

Alton came home from work one morning and told me that he had witnessed the printing of the declaration of war against Japan. We were awed by the sense of history and our part in it, but about this time Ole started bombarding us with letters begging us to come home. He had never learned to drive the tractor and was pretty helpless. I guess he must have thought his sons would always be there to do the farming for him, but Alton's two brothers had both been drafted, and Ole was finding it almost impossible to hire help. Neither of us wanted to go, but then came the telegrams. "Come home! Come home!" We were ready to give in when we discovered that I was pregnant. The doctor said I wasn't in any condition to travel, so once again we said "no" and avoided going back to Montana.

I wanted to work, and the Hecht Company was hiring, so I applied for and got a job in the warehouse. It wasn't much of a position, but I thought it would be exciting to work in the big city. I put an ad in the paper looking for a babysitter, and a pretty young girl applied. She had references and seemed nice, so I hired her. Alton stayed with Ricky for a couple of hours before he left for work so that he wouldn't be left with the girl for more than four hours. Ricky was good about it at first, but after a week or two, when he began to cry as I was getting ready to leave, I thought I had better ask some questions. He kept shaking his head when I asked him what the trouble was.

"She'll spank me if I tell," he said, and burst into tears. When I told him I would fire her and stay home with him myself, he finally told me how she hit him for no reason and locked him in the apartment and left him alone. I sometimes wonder if Ricky's imaginary friend "Jim," who showed up around that time, might have been the result of those days when I was working. At any rate, that was the end of my working outside the home.

We had a wonderful time together that year, but it wasn't all pleasure. One night in February there was a knock on the door in the middle of the night. I was afraid to open it because of all the crime in the neighborhood, but when I heard the word telegram and saw the envelope being pushed under the door I knew in my heart that it was about Mama.

"Mama died last night of a massive stroke," it said, and was signed Maribelle.

Mama, gone? She couldn't be. She was coming out for a visit next summer. Oh, Mama! I ran for the bathroom and retched until I couldn't get my breath.

Ricky woke and crawled into my lap. "Don't cry, Mama," he said, patting my cheek. "Don't cry."

I felt so alone waiting for Alton to come home from work. He badly needed his sleep, but he held me while I cried and we both fell asleep from exhaustion. The next evening I took Ricky and we walked to a nearby church where they were having an evening service. We waited in the back row until the congregation left, and I told the minister about my mother and asked if we could talk. He said he had a meeting to go to, but would come as soon as he could. He never showed up.

I cried a lot those next two weeks, and poor little Ricky could only say, "Don't cry, Mama," but he couldn't break through my grief. It must have been a bewildering time for him. I felt so guilty that I hadn't written more often, and then I found a letter that I had started writing and hadn't finished. "Dear Mama," it said. "I'm sorry to be so late with this letter. I miss you and think of you alone out there after all the years we spent together in schoolhouses. This is such an exciting place. Maybe together we can save enough for you to come on the train next summer. You will love it here. Ricky will be so glad to see you, and I can hardly wait." Now she would never know how much I loved her.

One night after Alton had left for work I began to have pains deep in my abdomen. They were hard grinding pains. Ricky woke up scared and began to cry, and I was scared, too, when I saw how much I was bleeding. It never occurred to me to call an ambulance, so I packed towels around myself and tried to calm Ricky while we waited for Alton to come home from work. The pain was excruciating, and sometime during the night I had a miscarriage. It was an extension of my agony over Mama's death.

There was nothing standing in the way now, so we began making plans to go back to Montana. Alton asked for a few days leave until I was feeling a little stronger and told them at work that he would be leaving the job. When he returned to work his boss approached him with an exciting offer. They were opening a subsidiary government printing office in St. Louis, Missouri, and wanted him to take the position as head printer. There would be a big raise in pay and a wonderful retirement plan. Again we had an important decision to make. We had almost decided to go to St. Louis when we received another phone call. Alton's brother had been seriously wounded in the Battle of the Bulge, and there was no longer any question about it. We had to go home.

We bought our tickets and started packing. Apartments were at such a premium that the renter agreed to take all of our furniture and paid us just what it had cost us. Meanwhile I made an appointment at a clinic down the street to see if I was alright after the miscarriage. I was put in a room, told to undress and slip into a paper gown and wait. I did as I was told, and an hour later a portly, officious little man came in. I was so cold that my teeth were chattering, and he made no apologies for keeping me waiting. Instead, he leaned close to me. "What did you do to get rid of it?" he asked.

I was horrified and started to cry, telling him through my sobs that I had wanted this baby and that I had just lost my mother, too. He sneered. "Don't pull that sob story on me,

Mrs. Sterry. I know all about little country girls who come to the big city and get into trouble. Well, get your knees up here and we'll see what we can do for you." I had my clothes on in minutes and was running through the office crying as he stood there with a loathsome look on his face.

I was glad we were going back. The city didn't seem as exciting and thrilling to me as it had a few months before.

Home Again

I had my childhood wish. I was married to my redheaded farmer, and we were back, back to hauling our water in a barrel, back to kerosene lamps, back to dirt and hot winds that sucked the moisture from our skin.

Rain was what we needed and, finally, rain was what we got in abundance. The garden flourished, the crops grew green and lovely, and our hopes were high. Ole and Maggie promised to give us the "north place" in exchange for our summer's work, a whole quarter section, and it looked as though we wouldn't regret our decision to come home. Ricky was so glad to see his grandma, and he had the whole world to roam in again. The old dog, Johnny, remembered him, and they were constant companions. He had also brought "Jimmy" home from Washington, D.C., with him. When Ricky got a cookie, Jimmy had to have one, too. At first I thought it was just a clever way of getting two cookies, but Jimmy was very real to him. I could often hear him talking and laughing as though he really had another little boy with him. He even made room for Jimmy at the supper table. Jimmy could share from his plate, he said.

Ricky was about to lose his first tooth. It seemed to be hanging by a thread, but he wouldn't let us pull it. All my stories about the tooth fairy wouldn't budge him until one day Alton had had enough. "I'm going to be home before dark, and you'd better have that tooth pulled before I get home, or I'm going to pull it for you," he said.

Ricky scowled. "Jimmy's daddy wouldn't make him pull his tooth, and I'm not going to pull mine, either!"

I talked him into letting me tie a string around it, but that was as far as I got. He went around with that string hanging from his mouth all afternoon, every so often giving it a dispirited little jerk. As evening approached we could see the tractor coming down the road, and Ricky was getting desperate. He would run out from behind the house every few minutes and peek to see how close his dad was, and then he'd duck around the back. The tractor pulled into the yard, and still the string hung from Ricky's mouth. Alton climbed down and started for the house and was almost there when Ricky gave a giant pull and ran to meet his dad with the tooth hanging from the string. I'm not certain, but I think that was when Jimmy left. Smart kid. He didn't want to stick around a place where a daddy made his little boy pull his own tooth.

One afternoon in July Alton came home and took Ricky to the field with him, "just for company," he said. It was almost dark and time for supper, and I was watching the east road for them to come home. I thought I saw the old Model T truck coming up the road, but it was so slow that I wasn't sure it was really moving. But, yes, there it was, getting closer as I watched. Strangely though, it didn't seem to have a driver. Still, it kept coming and turned the corner by the mailbox.

When the door flew open and six-year-old Ricky hopped out, all smiles, I couldn't believe my eyes. He put his hands in his pockets and strutted by me with a pleased look on his face. "What's for supper?" he said, in exactly his dad's tone of voice. Alton drove in with the pickup a few minutes later, and I was so mad I could have hit him with the grain shovel for taking such a chance. He explained that he had set the throttle so the truck could hardly move and told Ricky to stay between the ditches. "And he made it, didn't he?" he said.

Ricky was almost six years old when Craig was born, so he was his dad's only helper for too many years. When he grew up he was the only one of our boys who didn't want to have anything to do with farming. He was such a funny kid, though, and always seemed to know what would make me laugh. He avoided a lot of trouble that way. Once, when Alton took him to town for a haircut, the barber asked him if he was a good Norwegian like his daddy. "No, Mama says I have a little Irish in me," Ricky said. When the barber asked where the Irish was, Ricky said, "I think it's my tongue."

I bought his coveralls a size too big and rolled up the sleeves and pant legs. He always wanted to be older, so when Mrs. Kersey asked him how old he was, he pulled the label around where she could see it. "It says right here someplace," he said.

Alton and I had our squabbles as all couples do, and sharing a house without plumbing or electricity with his parents didn't help matters. There was one time Alton went too far, though, and it almost ended our marriage. We had had a rain shower, and he couldn't work in the field for the rest of the day. It was always a time for rejoicing when it rained, even if it was just a little shower. It meant we could get away from the daily grind for a little while.

Alton wanted to go to town for a haircut and a few beers with the guys, and I wanted to go to the movies since we had a built-in baby sitter in Maggie. I gave in when he promised to be home by suppertime and take me to the show. So I killed a chicken and made his favorite meal, chicken and dumplings. I took a bath and washed and set my hair, looking forward to my evening out. When he hadn't come home by suppertime I knew I wouldn't get to go to the movies. I put the dinner in the oven to keep warm and an hour later still thought he'd be there any minute.

Ole drove into the yard about then and started speaking Norwegian to Maggie, which he knew infuriated me. I heard Alton's name mentioned, and then the name of the bachelor who lived a few miles from us. This bachelor neighbor was known to bring a "working girl" out from Havre on occasion.

"You might as well put supper on the table," Ole snickered. "He won't be here to eat it, I can guarantee that."

I was already spitting mad, and this was the last straw. "Supper's in the oven," I snarled and rushed upstairs.

When Alton walked in a couple of hours later I lit into him, screeching like a scalded cat, right in front of Ole and Maggie.

He didn't say a word, but he had a white line around his mouth. He let me carry on for a few minutes, then turned and grabbed me. Out the door we went, with me over his shoulder.

"Where are you taking me?" I yelled.

"Are you going to shut up?"

"No," I screamed, and he headed for the rain barrel.

"Now will you shut up?"

When I hollered "no" again, he ducked me into the barrel head first and then pulled me out gasping and sputtering. Then he ducked me one more time for good measure.

I swore I wouldn't speak to him for a month, and I almost made it through the next day. He apologized and confessed that he had been at the bachelor's place. He'd only stopped in for one drink, had had another, and then every time he'd made a move to leave someone would hand him another drink. He was sorry and ashamed, and I learned that day how powerful forgiveness can be. We went to the show the next night, and Alton's folks moved to town soon after. Of course we got mad at each other many times in the years ahead, but Alton never again touched me in anger.

Hail and Farewell

When Maribelle came to Havre from Cut Bank for Memorial Day in 1942, we visited Mama's grave together. The sky was gray, and we left an armful of roses on Mama's tombstone, but we both agreed that the abandoned one-room schoolhouses all over Montana were Mama's real monuments. She gave her life to those schools and to the many children who were inspired by her example.

Maribelle and I hadn't had a chance to visit since I had returned from Washington, D.C. "What happened to Mama's things?" I asked her. "Didn't I tell you about that?" she said. "We went out to her school right after the funeral, and all of her possessions were gone—the oak rocker, her brass bedstead, and the sewing machine, even her little radio. Her clothes were ripped off the hangers and thrown on the floor. We did salvage one thing, though," she said. "In an old shoe box we found a ragged dishtowel, and rolled up inside were the baby moccasins Mama had kept all these years."

I missed Mama desperately, and there was still some tension between Alton's parents and us: While they told us they were planning to find a place in town, they never seemed to get around to it. More significantly, they had promised to let us buy the farm if we came back, but once we returned, Maggie began to wonder aloud what Delos, Alton's brother, would have to look forward to when he recovered from his war wounds and came home. Just two more years of college and Alton could go back to teaching school, while Delos didn't have an education. We could understand her position and hoped Alton could go back to school with the proceeds from that first crop. We spent a great deal of time looking at the sky and trying to outguess the weather that summer, and there was a lot of anxiety. That's life on a dry land farm, though, and I never regretted marrying a farmer.

Meanwhile Ole and I continued to aggravate each other. He had an old blue Chevrolet that he was very proud of, but he never quite got the hang of driving it, and he was a menace on the road. He did everything but yell "giddy-up" and "whoa," and the idea of his wife or daughters learning to drive was beyond his comprehension. I had another key made, though, and took Maggie for a ride every chance I got. Word got back to me that he had grumbled about me to one of his McNess customers. "That daughter-in-law of mine," he said, "she's just like Mrs. Roosevelt. She just gets in the car and goes."

By fall the wheat looked beautiful. We had never seen it so perfect, and we started adding up bushels to the acre, and figuring on the back of envelopes, but the old saying, "don't count your chickens before they're hatched," means don't count your bushels before they're harvested, either. When the hail came, it came straight down, the size of golf balls. Alton was as white as the hail when we drove to the north place to find the wheat just a green pulp, running in rivers down the field. Our hopes for the future washed away with the wheat.

Within two weeks we received a letter from Maribelle. Her husband, Bob, had been drafted. She had decided to go to California so she could be near him while he was in basic training, and Bob's Safeway store needed a produce man. He suggested that Alton apply for the job. We drove to Cut Bank, and he was hired on the spot. Again I was in housekeeper heaven. We rented a cute little two-bedroom furnished house. Ricky found new friends to play with, and I was happy. I didn't get too settled, as I knew we would be going back to the farm in the spring. That was pretty much the way I had lived all my life, never putting down roots, and I wanted a stable life more than anything.

We were happy when we found that I was pregnant again. We would have a new baby in August 1943. I felt wonderful all during that pregnancy, and it never occurred to me that I might have trouble with the new baby's birth. We left Cut Bank April 1 and were soon settled into the routine of farm work. The days were long and hard for Alton, who put in fifteen-hour days that summer. But Ricky was glad to be home again, and his grandma was happy to see him.

One afternoon in the middle of August, I had just finished making a batch of doughnuts when a car full of my old school friends drove up. We had a great time reminiscing and eating doughnuts. When it was time to leave, one of the women decided she should stay. I wasn't worried and told her so. It was two weeks until my delivery time, but I couldn't talk her out of it. She said she just had a feeling she would be needed.

Alton had gone to town for some machinery repairs, but I expected him home before dark. When he didn't show up, we put Ricky to bed and went to bed ourselves. I was awakened about midnight with contractions. We timed them to be sure and then wrapped Ricky up in a blanket and headed for town with my friend driving the Model A. There was a big harvest moon that night, and it was a good thing, as the lights flickered and went out before we reached the gravel road. Alton was headed home, and we met him at the railroad tracks. After settling Rick with Grandma and dropping my friend off, he and I set out for Havre as fast as the little car would go.

Alton apologized all the way for not getting home when he said he would, but I was happy to be having the baby and was in a forgiving mood. We needn't have hurried, though; the baby wasn't born until eight the next night. Alton kept coming to the hospital and rapping on the delivery room door to see if his baby had been born, and then going back downtown to the Elks Club. Apparently, the guys at the bar would toast the new papa every time he came back with no news. The last time he opened the delivery room door he stepped inside with a big silly grin on his face and tried to give me a ragged bouquet of flowers.

As the young nurse hustled him out the door he yelled, "I picked 'em just for you, honey, and I'm not leaving 'til we get our baby."

It must have had some effect, because the doctor showed up and delivered the baby with forceps. He was a perfect little boy with only two pink spots where the forceps had been. The next day there was talk among the nurses about the bare spot in the hospital flowerbed. Only the delivery room nurse and I knew why, and we weren't telling.

St. Elmo's Fire

We named our new baby Craig Robert and prepared for as happy and easy a child as Rick had been. Nothing could have been farther from reality. Craig cried constantly. He had caught impetigo while in the hospital, and we discovered later, after days of crying and regurgitating his milk, that he had pyloric stenosis, a condition that should have been corrected right after his birth. He suffered from chronic stomach pains until he was eight years old.

It wasn't too long until I was pregnant again, and I worried about whether I could meet the challenge of two little ones in diapers, especially given Craig's health and the timing of my due date. I knew Alton would help me with the kids once harvest was over, but I wouldn't be able to count on much support until September. Ole and Maggie had moved to town, and while I was glad we weren't living on top of each other anymore, I missed Maggie's help with the kids.

It was late July and I was getting pretty uncomfortable with the new baby's birth only a couple of weeks away, but because it was harvest, I had to keep working. Nothing came easily. It seemed as though every time I got the car loaded with lunches and headed for the field, the engine would belch, cough a few times, and stop just before my destination. Sometimes Alton would come looking for me, mad and hungry. The car always started right up for him.

My worst mistake was when I couldn't find the field where the men were combining. I could hear the machinery, but I couldn't see the combine. I didn't want to just start out carrying Craig, who still couldn't walk, when I didn't know which direction to take. I finally turned around and drove home, figuring that when they got hungry enough someone would come and look for me. They did come to get the lunch, hungry and mad, and I never was allowed to forget it. That's how the "hidden field" got its name.

Once, after I brought the afternoon lunch out, Alton told me he was going to work late, and I was supposed to come out to the field at midnight to bring him home. Naturally I thought it would be the same general direction. He had neglected to tell me that he was going to the north field, and I wandered around looking for him about twelve miles from where he was. He gave up on me and walked the six miles home, and we both got home at the same time. He was pretty mad, but he had to admit that he hadn't told me where he would be. He had the last word, though. "You could have followed my tracks!" he said. It was a totally moonless night. You can always tell a Norwegian, but you can't tell him much!

The times the car would sputter to a stop and I had to walk the last mile home were the worst, carrying Craig over my bulging stomach, in the dust and heat, with the air filled with flying grasshoppers. At least I thought it was the worst until we got caught in a downpour on our way to the north place. Alton had pulled the machinery up there and needed a ride home. The sky had darkened and the clouds were a rolling black mass. Thunder boomed and lightning cracked and the sky opened up with a sheet of rain. Craig woke up and discovered that his bottle was empty and was crying at the top of his voice, and then the windshield wiper quit—just as I bounced into a rut—and stayed there. Although I tried every trick I had seen Alton use to get out of the mud, it was no use. I was stuck.

Greeno's farmhouse was about three-quarters of a mile away, so I wrapped my coat around Craig, settled him over the bulge, and started walking. I was only about a fourth of the way when blue fire the size of a tennis ball came bouncing across the road in front of me. I froze in my tracks, not knowing which way to go. Suddenly blue balls were all around me, bouncing from fence to fence. It was one of the most beautiful and most frightening sights I have ever seen. Then, just as suddenly as they had come, they disappeared. Years later someone told me that it was a phenomenon called St. Elmo's fire. I'm told that it has something to do with dust particles, dry air, and electricity combined with moisture.

We must have been a sorry-looking sight as we turned into the farmer's yard. Far ahead I could see another lone figure walking in the downpour, and I knew Alton was on his way. Mrs. Greeno met us at the door with a warm blanket and sent her husband to get Alton. Craig had a warm bottle of milk, and I had my feet in a pan of warm water and was drinking a cup of tea when the men came in the door. I know Alton was furious, but when he saw what a bedraggled mess I was, he felt almost as sorry for me as I did for myself.

The blazing hot day we brought Alan home from the hospital we stopped to pick up Craig and Ricky from Maggie and Ole's place in town. Alton admitted that things were pretty much of a mess at home, and he couldn't help me since he was needed in the field. Of course I knew that, and I certainly wouldn't have planned a harvest birth if I could have helped it. But believe me, there wasn't going to be another hunting trip for Alton in November, not if I had anything to say about it.

Obviously harvest was not a good time to bring a new baby to the farm. Maggie had been pressed into service to cook, and she was not happy about it. One year, maybe, but two harvest babies in two years? And it was the hottest August I can remember. The house was worse than I expected when I got home. My mother-in-law had left an awful mess, especially for a young mother with a new baby and another child still in diapers. The kitchen was full of dirty dishes, the laundry basket full of dirty diapers, and there was no water. There was no other way to handle it, so I left six-year-old Ricky to watch the babies while I ran down to the well for enough water to get supper, and Alton did come in early and bring up a barrel of water for washing. We were barely in the door when Ole came driving up with a load of wheat.

"They want some coffee out there, Alton," he said, and then to me, "What have you got for lunch?" Alton could see that I was about to explode, so he hustled his dad out the door, saying he would bring something out later. That was probably the worst harvest season in my memory.

Rocky Boy

We were just finishing the harvest when a strange car drove into the yard. Two men came to the door and said they had a proposition for Alton. They were from the Rocky Boy Indian Agency. Their shop teacher had been drafted, and they had heard that Alton might be available. He told them he had never taught shop and only held a two-year teaching certificate. That didn't matter, they said. They also needed a basketball coach and knew he would fill the bill. They explained that there was a new house for the teacher. It had two bedrooms and new maple furniture. There was a bottle-gas stove and refrigerator. There was a full basement with a washing machine. We only had to bring our personal belongings.

Alton protested that he had fall work.

"Take whatever time you need," they told him. "When can you be there?"

"Okay. I'll give it a try," Alton said. "But I can't make it before October 1."

I could hardly believe my good fortune. We had only six weeks to get ready, and it took a lot of work. Olaf and I helped pick rock while Maggie took care of the kids, and in my spare time, I packed box after box. I was sure that we would need more than just our personal belongings.

So there we were in mid-afternoon on October 1, 1943, with Ricky and Craig in the back seat surrounded by boxes of diapers and blankets and cooking pans. I held two-month-old Alan, and we were on our way. Dark clouds were coming in from the north by the time we reached Box Elder and headed toward the Rocky Boy Reservation. Thunder rolled and lightning shattered the sky as it began to rain, and we slipped and slid around those hairpin turns through the Bear's Paw Mountains. Then with a cough and a sputter, the engine died. Alton got out and raised the hood. I watched while the rain filled his hat brim and ran down his neck. The babies were crying, and we were all hungry. He tinkered with the engine and said it probably just needed to cool off. He was right, and after a short rest, he tried the starter and we were on our way again.

Alton's face was flushed and hot when he tried to help me carry the most necessary things into our new house. He was shaking so hard he could hardly walk. The school superintendent drove in right behind us. "Well, here you are," he said, "but I can see you're in no condition to work, so we'll just postpone school until we get you back on your feet. I'll call the nurse right now."

The nurse helped me make up the bed and then gave Alton a shot for the flu, but it took three days for him to recover enough to get out of bed. Meanwhile, I got Ricky registered at the school in Box Elder. We had hoped that he would be attending the reservation school, but it appeared that was against the rules. It would be a long tiring ride for a first grader.

Alton was still weak, but said he was ready for his first day of school. He was pretty nervous when he left that morning, and it was worse than he thought it would be. He was greeted by a classroom full of sullen kids who didn't like being cooped up inside, didn't like school, and didn't like their young redheaded teacher. The basketball team was made up of natural athletes, so Alton enjoyed that part of his job better than he thought he would.

The shop class, though, was a different story. The students remained hostile and uncooperative. One morning when Alton unlocked the door to the shop, he discovered that all of the expensive tools were missing. He was heartsick, but he couldn't let them get away with it. When the class assembled he told them that since this was government property the theft was a federal offense, and if the tools weren't returned within twenty-four hours, he would have to notify the FBI. He told them that he knew it was just a prank and hated the thought of any of those young men spending time in prison, so if the tools were returned by the next morning, he wouldn't report it, and it would never be mentioned again. He was bluffing, and he knew it, but they didn't, and all of the tools were piled against the door in the morning. From that time on, those fierce kids were his staunchest supporters.

Craig kept me busy. He was just learning to walk, but he could climb anyplace, and I had all I could do to keep him from hurting himself while I took care of Ricky and the baby. One of Craig's favorite places was the floor-to-ceiling cupboards. He would pull out the drawers to use for steps and climb up to get the butter or brown sugar, his favorite treat. We had a floor furnace, and one morning when I was making Ricky's school lunch I heard Craig scream. He had walked bare-footed onto its grill and had a pattern of burns across the bottoms of both feet. I knew there was no way we could keep him from walking on them, so I wrapped his feet in diapers and padded them well, and they healed without breaking a blister.

Since Alton was often away for a game with the basketball team, I was at home alone with the children quite a lot. I was never lonely and never afraid to be alone, but one time my courage was put to the test. Ricky was staying over with a friend that Friday night, so I was home alone with the two little ones. It had started raining right after the school bus left that morning, and the rain came down relentlessly all day long. The road just below our house was slick with gumbo, and no one ventured out on it until nearly time for supper. It had been a boring day, and I watched idly out the window as a battered pickup truck slipped and slid erratically, stopping and starting with much grinding of gears. Finally it slid into the ditch, up to its fenders in mud.

I heard screaming and cursing as the pickup door flew open and a woman was pushed out into the ditch. I opened my door a crack and could hear her screams as a man jumped out and began beating and kicking her. With a last kick he turned and lurched up the road in the direction of the country store, a half mile away. The woman slowly dragged herself up the bank, and with blood streaming down her face, headed for our house. She pounded on the door. "Let me in!" She yelled. "Save me. My husband is trying to kill me."

I was in a panic, afraid to let her in and still unable to leave her outside in the rain, possibly to bleed to death. As I opened the door a strong whiff of stale whiskey came in with her, and soon the chair I gave her was covered with mud and blood as she swayed back and forth, moaning. I tried to call the reservation nurse, but got no answer. It was up to me to clean her up as best I could. Craig had awakened from his nap and was standing big-eyed in the doorway, beginning to screw up his face to cry. I took time to quiet him and gave him a cracker and then went to work trying to clean the woman's wounds. "My husband, he's a mean man. He will get you for helping me now," she said when I had finished.

"What do you mean, get me?" I asked.

She shrugged. "I dunno. Beat you up. Kill you. Something, I guess."

I tried again to reach the nurse, but still no answer. The woman was now standing at the window with her back to me, muttering. Suddenly she said, "There he comes."

I ran to look and, sure enough, the man was staggering down the road from the store. Craig had finished his cracker and had started to cry again, and this time Alan joined him. I flew around locking windows and doors to the sound of crying babies and a muttered "Better watch out," from the woman.

I kept trying the nurse's number but still no answer. The man had reached his pickup and was rummaging around in it, probably for his bottle. Then he stared a long time at our house and started slowly up the hill toward us. He was nearly to the sidewalk when I pulled the blinds, and then I remembered the basement windows. I flew down the stairs, pulled up a crate, and locked one window and was reaching for the latch on the other one when I saw his pant legs outside. I pulled the latch just as he bent over to look. There we were, face to face. He knocked and made motions for me to let him in as I backed away and ran up the stairs. Now there was a great banging on the door, and he began to prowl around the house, trying each window. I raced to the phone to try again to reach the nurse.

This time, blessedly, she answered. I only needed to tell her who I was, and she recognized the fear in my voice and said she would be right there. The man started to walk away, and I breathed a sigh of relief, but when he bent and picked up a large rock I knew he meant to break the window. My prayers were answered as the nurse's car turned the corner and headed up the hill.

She took in the situation at a glance, and after a few words to the man gave him a push in the direction of the pickup, and he shambled off.

"Well, Mary," the nurse said as she looked the woman over. "I see you and Ben are at it again."

Mary grinned sheepishly. "Yah. We gotta get drunk and fight sometimes I guess." Then, as she followed the nurse out the door, she turned to me. "My Ben, he's gonna get you for helping me," she said. "He's a real mean man."

My experience that rainy evening became the subject for a lot of laughs from the Rocky Boy staff, I heard later. "Ben wouldn't hurt a soul," they said, but I was there, and to me it had all the ingredients of a tragedy waiting to happen. Maybe I was just lucky. I heard years later that Ben was serving time for assault. I never heard if the victim was Mary or some other unlucky person.

We stayed another term, and Alton was asked to take the job permanently. He would need two more quarters of college, which they would pay for. We seriously considered it, but then Ole offered to sell us the farm, and Alton decided to accept his offer. I can't help wondering what our lives would have been like if he had accepted the printer's job in St. Louis or the Rocky Boy position. I guess the road not traveled will always make us wonder.

The Girdle

During the war years we were lucky if we could find any clothes to buy. I bought a stack of faded striped men's overalls in the local store for twenty-five cents apiece, ripped them apart, and turned them inside out for overalls for the little boys. My sewing machine was a godsend those years.

We had a secondhand davenport and chair that had seen much better days, and I decided to upholster them. I sent for a "how-to" booklet and a kit of tools from the Sears catalog and set to work ripping the furniture apart. I got the material from Buttreys in Havre. There wasn't much to choose from, and this particular material was heavy and smelled a little like diesel fuel. The salesman said the smell was from the packing box, but it would go away. Besides, he would give it to me for half price. The material had a cloth backing and was a particularly odious shade of maroon, but never one to pass up a bargain, I bought it. My old treadle machine got a real workout, and I eventually got the two pieces of furniture finished. I even re-tied the springs, and I think I was prouder of that than anything I had ever tried to do.

They told me at the store when I bought the material that it would wear like iron. It did, and it felt a lot like iron when you sat on it, too—cold and stiff. I think we would have had to use it forever if mice hadn't gotten into it one cat-less winter. Maybe the smell from the material made them sick, but it wasn't long before the unmistakable odor of dead mice overpowered the already strong odor of the davenport and chair. We cleaned it out as best we could and tried to live with it, but there was no question that we would have to replace the set and bring in one or two of the barn cats. I didn't weep any tears over it.

We farmers lived well during the war years. We raised pigs and cured our own hams and bacon and had a cow for milk and butter. The cow was a fence-crawler and a thorn in Alton's flesh from the day he brought her home. She always had cuts and scratches on her legs and udder, and she wouldn't let me near her, so I never learned to milk properly. I tried and tried, but the old cow wouldn't let down her milk for me. She would lean on me and invariably put her foot in the milk pail or kick me, so Alton had to milk her when he got home from the field.

I always had a big kettle of sour milk on the back of the stove to make into cottage cheese the next day. I poured off the whey, put the curds in a flour sack, and pinned it to the clothesline, and the next morning it was the best cottage cheese in the world. It was so different from the kind we get in the stores today as it was made with thick cream and no preservatives. We hadn't heard the word "cholesterol" and enjoyed it without a qualm. In spite of rationing we lived well, with our own canned beef and chicken. We had no refrigeration, but the canned meat was delicious, though I remember what a treat it was when we were able to buy some bologna with our ration stamps.

We had a big garden. Ole always planted several rows of corn, and we had lots of fried chicken, new potatoes and peas, and corn on the cob in time for harvest. It was next to impossible to get a hired man, so Maggie would come out from Hingham with Ole. She cooked and watched the kids while Ole, Rick, Alton, and I were the harvest crew. I was up at six, making pies, buns, and potato salad and putting up a lunch to take to the field. Ricky and I took turns on the tractor, and then Ricky finished off the day while I went home to help make supper. After supper everyone except the cook went to bed. I would still be up doing dishes at eleven. I sound like I'm complaining, but I liked getting out of the house and away from the kids for a while.

I was out of clean clothes one fateful morning and gave Alton a new chambray shirt to wear. The north field was always the last of the harvest, and tempers were getting short by then, especially when the dark clouds started rolling in. It was there that

Alton almost lost his arm. Ricky was driving the tractor that pulled the combine. Ole was driving the grain truck, and Alton was riding the new pull-type case combine which had rows of sharp knives that cut the wheat. I had just come out to the field with afternoon lunch and everything was going smoothly when Alton leaned over to pull something out of the header and his sleeve got caught. When Ricky heard his dad yell, it startled him, and he let go of the clutch on the tractor, dragging Alton along and pulling him in tighter. Ole began to jump up and down and scream at Ricky until he finally got the tractor stopped, and the three of them got Alton free of the machine. If he had been wearing one of his old shirts it would have torn free. I never again sent anyone to the field in anything but old, worn-out clothes.

Alton was white and shaky, and we both knew he had broken a rib or two. He could barely take a breath, but he wouldn't go see a doctor. "Can't you see that big cloud? It's either rain, now that we don't need it, or wind," he said. "We can't leave until we finish this field, and I don't have time to argue."

Nevertheless, I tried to argue, and he was furious with me.

"Just go on home and get one of your girdles," he said, "and bring some scissors."

I knew I couldn't change his mind, so I drove back to the house and got my girdle. We cut it off so it just fit around his ribs, and he was in agony as we helped him pull that girdle on, but he got right back on the combine again. The way they made a woman's girdle in those days, he couldn't have found anything more unyielding. He wore that thing until the fall work was done and was in misery the whole time. Alton always got a rash during harvest, and this year it was worse than ever with that girdle chafing him. I began giving him back rubs and foot massages after his bath so he could get some sleep, and he really appreciated it. I didn't know how much until he took me to Great Falls for an overnight shopping trip after harvest and told me I could buy myself something special.

"Just let me sleep," he said, "and you can buy anything you want—within reason, of course."

He never should have said that. There was a music store just two blocks away from our motel, and the proprietor showed me a secondhand Hammond spinet organ with a complete set of self-help lessons. "Only eight hundred dollars," he said. I admired it but knew it was not really "within reason." By noon Alton was ready to get up, and I took him to the music shop. When we left I was the owner of an organ I didn't know how to play. I couldn't even read notes. I burned the bottom out of a whole set of pans while I was trying to learn the chords that winter. I couldn't walk by the organ without sitting down to play, and time would slip by until I smelled the potatoes burning. It's a wonder I didn't burn the house down.

Turkey Talk

In 1947 the Rural Electrical Association changed our lives by bringing power to the farm. For me that meant an electric iron, range, and refrigerator. I rarely stopped smiling that first electrified summer. It was a happy year. That April, I went to the hospital resigned to having another boy. Instead, I finally got my baby girl, and I was delirious with joy. She had dimples and big blue eyes, and I know she smiled at me when the nurse brought her in for the first time. She was perfect.

Strangely, after all those years of hoping for a girl, I hadn't picked out a girl's name. All the nurses and even the doctor kept nagging me to name the baby so they could fill out her birth certificate. I couldn't think of a single name I felt right about. The nurses began to bully me, but I wouldn't budge. Then one night in a dream, Mama suggested that I name her Sandra Louise since that was the name I would have given Ricky if he had been a girl. The next day there was rejoicing in the maternity ward. Baby Girl Sterry was now Sandra Louise Sterry.

I was so excited at having my little girl that my blood pressure leaped into the stroke level. Just after I was told that I could go home the next day, I felt a strange sensation. I was alone in my room when I felt as though the bed was rising off the floor. I was floating just under the ceiling when a nurse came in, took my blood pressure, and went running down the hall. She came back with a doctor and another nurse. They gave me a shot, and the nurse stayed close the rest of the day. After a consultation they decided to keep me a little longer. They put a "no visitors" sign on my door and wouldn't even let my brother and his wife in to see me. Sandra Louise and I were there for twelve days, and the baby was sleeping through the night and waking up with dry diapers when I got her home. The nurses had trained her well.

Sandra was a delightful child, sweet, loving, quiet, and thoughtful. She could be stubborn, though, like her Grandma Maggie, who only insisted on having her way when she knew she was in the right, or so she always said. I thought I would never spank my children and rarely did, but once I swatted Sandra on the behind for something and felt awful about it. I hugged her and said I was sorry and asked to kiss and make up, but she just gave me a stony look. "No. I'd ruther be mad," she said.

She had honey-blond hair, and unlike me, had lots of it. I loved braiding and curling Sandra's hair and sewing pretty dresses for her. I had my little blue-eyed, golden-haired doll at last. It wasn't a role she took to, though. When she started school, I would send her off dressed in a sweater and skirt, knee socks and shiny shoes, every hair in place, and she would come tearing off the bus that afternoon with her socks baggy and twisted, her slip hanging, her sweater buttoned crooked, wearing a big grin. "Guess what, Mama," she would say, "I hit a home run today!" Sandra wanted to do everything the boys did and loved sports.

Sandra was my only helper, but she would far rather have been working in the field with her brothers than doing housework. She never quite forgave her dad when her girlfriends got to drive the grain trucks for harvest and she didn't. She got tired of hearing people tell her to be a good girl and help her mother.

I remember the time I talked the boys into chipping in on a pretty little wristwatch for her birthday. There was a radio station that had a birthday program. They would announce the name of the birthday child and then tell the child where to look for a present. I sent her name in, and we all listened when the program came on the air. "Happy birthday, Sandra Sterry," the announcer said. "If you want to find your birthday present, go look in your mother's sewing basket." Her face fell, and she raced upstairs looking like a thundercloud. Our little tomboy had been hoping for a fishing rod, and she knew it would never fit into a sewing basket, but after her friends at school admired her new watch, she wore it proudly.

Sandra's birthdays were nearly always a disappointment to her. She passionately wanted to own a horse, and her faith was strong. Year after year she would look in vain for her horse and even decided one time that we had gotten her a Shetland pony and hidden it in her room upstairs. Alton thought it was time to do something about her longing and borrowed a horse from a neighbor. He told Sandra that if she took care of it for a month, and learned to ride, he would buy her a horse of her own.

Sandra and the horse took an instant dislike to each other. It was a love affair gone wrong from the start, and feeding and watering him was Sandra's job. Every time she got near him he would try to bite her, or back her against the fence, and she would come in mad and red-faced, but she never admitted to any of us how disappointed she was. This went on for two weeks, and we were afraid the horse would hurt her, so Alton returned it to its owner. The day she came home from school to find the pasture empty was a day to celebrate. Alton could always figure his girls out better than I could.

Sandra was about five the spring I decided it was time for the boys to have bikes. Alton said we couldn't afford them, but I came up with a plan that I was later to regret. I would raise turkeys and sell them to all our friends for a tidy profit. Voila— the boys would have their bikes, and we would also have our Thanksgiving turkey. How difficult could it be? Alton reluctantly agreed, and we were soon to find out just how difficult.

Turkeys are doubtless the stupidest of domesticated animals. They smell bad, they're noisy, and nothing is safe from their ex- crement. The truck, the tractor, the car, and the pickup all were liberally coated. And they loved the combine. To them it was a large mother turkey we had thoughtfully provided for them to snuggle up to.

Alton was mad all summer because of those creatures. Sandra was just getting old enough so I could let her go out and play by herself for a short time, and the turkeys would follow her every place she went. I watched her from the window as she headed for the swings with her doll in a box held up over her head. There they'd be, chirking and gobbling and stretching their necks, trying to see what was in the box. No matter how often I chased them away, they always came right back, but Sandra was just as determined as they were. She wanted to take her dolly on the swing, and she wasn't going to let them stop her.

Those turkeys were everywhere. To make matters worse, their heads swelled up, adding to their nastiness. An old turkey grower told us it was sinusitis. He said we'd have to lance the bags of fluid hanging under their eyes if we expected them to grow up to grace our table and those of our friends for Thanksgiving. One night Alton announced that we would be getting up an hour early to get the dirty job done before the kids left for school. Cries of "Aw, Dad," were heard, but we needed all the help we could get. I had never been known to do things by halves, and there were two dozen turkeys, all afflicted with sinusitis. The kids and I chased the turkeys into a corner of the chicken yard and then took turns sitting on them while Alton performed the surgery.

What a mess! Before they were through the kids all needed a change of clothes. It was mayhem. The toms were gobbling and the hens were chirking and running in every direction. In their panic the birds managed to defecate on anything they came into contact with, and essence of turkey was everywhere. The kids were mortified when the school bus arrived and had to wait for them while they washed and changed their clothes.

Raising the flock was bad enough, but butchering and preparing them for market was another ordeal, all of which fell upon Alton. I offered to help, but when I saw the heartless way it was done I couldn't even stay and watch. I had butchered hundreds of chickens and thought I could help butcher the turkeys. You don't scald and pluck them the same way you do chickens, I discovered. Each bird was hung in the garage by its feet and had its throat slit and its large feathers stripped off while it bled to death. I was given the job of plucking the pinfeathers, and I promised myself that I would never again come up with another plan for raising money.

I don't remember how many of the flock we raised to maturity, but I do know that we sold them all except three. There were two turkeys left for us and one for our friend and neighbor, George. He wasn't in a hurry to take his home, and the turkey grew to weigh thirty-five pounds. Nobody loved a party more than George, and we knew a party was in the making when he saw that big bird. "Sterry," he said. "It's time to butcher him."

The turkey was too big for an ordinary oven, so George had to cook him in Mrs. Kersey's hotel oven. He invited all his friends and it was, as we knew it would be, a party to remember. When dinner was over, we pushed the tables back. Some of us danced to the radio and others played cards while Alton and George settled down to do some serious drinking. They opened a bottle of gin and set it between them and began quoting from Poe's "The Raven." They disagreed on a couple of lines, and while they were looking for the book of poetry, George's wife Jean and I switched bottles. We flavored it a little with half a cup of gin and filled the bottle with water. They spent the rest of the evening taking turns swigging from the bottle and reading Poe and never knew the difference. When it was time to go home, Alton handed me the keys and said, "I'm shorry honey, but you'll have to drive home. I'm juss too drunk to try it." George and Alton refused to believe us when we told them they had been drinking water all night.

The kids got their bikes, but the turkey episode took the edge off our enthusiasm. I don't think they had ever been as excited about them as I was anyway. My dream as a child was someday to have a bike of my own, and, by gosh, they were going to have bikes and enjoy them or I'd know the reason why.

The turkey story wasn't quite over. Alton had butchered the extra one of ours at the same time he did George's, and it was taking up a lot of room in the freezer. It was time to butcher a beef, and he needed the freezer space, so I decided to have another turkey party. Alton objected. "It's too much work," he said.

"You'll wear yourself out for a bunch of people who won't even appreciate it."

In spite of Alton's objections I went ahead and sent out invitations. It was a big turkey, but it would fit in our oven. The rest of the planning could be done later. I was going to be the grandest hostess in Hingham and was planning a party that would outdo even George's, with three tables of bridge after dinner. Unfortunately, one of the couples I invited couldn't come, so I had to invite a couple that was every hostess's nightmare. The wife was convinced that her husband was the prize catch of the Hi-Line and was sure that most of the other women thought so, too. She had been known to drag him from the dance floor if she thought he was dancing too close with some unlucky woman. She could get pretty ornery at the bridge table, too, but I needed them to fill out a table.

It was a lot of work getting ready, but I wanted to prove to Alton that I could do it. I worked for three days cooking and baking, and then, just for good measure, after stuffing the turkey and putting it in the oven at five a.m., I got the family ready, and we went to church at nine. On the way back from church I reviewed my plans. There wasn't much to be done. The table was set, the turkey would be luscious and brown, the vegetables were ready, and all I had to do was make the gravy and salad.

I was mentally patting myself on the back when we drove into the yard, but when we opened the door we knew something was wrong. We didn't smell turkey. I raced across the kitchen and opened the oven. It was cold and the turkey was raw. This was our brand-new bottled gas stove, and the steel griddle and four burners were still working, but the oven flame had burned out. I turned and looked into Alton's "I told you so" eyes and burst into tears. The guests would begin to arrive in an hour, but Alton came through as he always had. "We have just enough steaks in the freezer," he said. "I'll get them to thawing."

I was saved. As the guests began to arrive we explained what had happened, and they were gracious about it. All of them, that is, except the guest from hell. "Good heavens," she said, "we came out here for turkey. We raise beef, and we can have steaks anytime." Then with a disdainful glance at the cupboard full of thawing steaks—"We might as well go home."

Her husband had been embarrassed by her before and would doubtless be again. "I'm looking forward to a good meal and an afternoon of bridge. We're staying," he said.

I know it didn't measure up to George's, but everyone declared it a great party. There was only one dissenter. She complained that the steak was tough, the house was either too hot or too cold, and she had terrible cards all afternoon.

The New Kitchen

I knew it was going to be "one of those days" the minute I opened my eyes. There was a heavy stillness to the air, a sort of foreboding. I lay there savoring the quiet, knowing it wouldn't last. Turning off the alarm, I watched Alton snuggle down deeper into the covers. Enjoy it while you can, I thought. In little more than a month, when spring work started, he would be back to fifteen-hour workdays.

It was time to get Ricky up. I hugged him and wished him happy birthday and thought he felt a little hot. He said he felt fine, and I wrote it off as excitement over the Valentine's Day party at school. I could already hear Alan and Craig shrieking as they jumped into bed with Alton. No more sleep for him.

The new baby, Sandra, woke crying and wouldn't take her bottle, and there was more than the usual bedlam getting everyone fed and Ricky off for school. I watched as the school bus turned the corner and noticed that the sky was getting darker and that it looked like snow over the Sweet Grass Hills. They were our measuring stick, those hills, the only break in the horizon. In the winter, touched by the westering sun, they looked like a handful of opals tossed on velvet. Stories were told about families who started out on a sunny summer day with an afternoon picnic in mind, only to discover that the distance was deceiving, and they were not to reach home again until well after dark.

The lean-to kitchen had been pulled away from the old homestead, and a new addition was being built along the north side of the house. It was unfinished and waiting for the carpenter, who was expected any day. The big cook stove, the cupboard, cream separator, table, and chairs were all crammed into the living room. There were only two rooms downstairs and one large room upstairs—a sort of barracks—where the boys slept. With the baby's crib in the main room downstairs, it made for tight maneuvering.

By noon the wind was whistling around the eaves, and the snow was beginning to come down in a slanting sheet. Looking out the window, I saw a strange car coming up the road, and as I watched, it turned into the yard. A stout lady got out, followed by Ricky. She banged officiously on the door and showed me a quarantine sign. "Your boy has scarlet fever," she said in an accusing voice, "and you will be quarantined for a month."

It was impossible, of course. I explained to her that we couldn't be quarantined because we had a carpenter coming to remodel our house. She listened and shook her head. There was nothing she could do. Then the nurse heard the baby's strangling cough. "She has whooping cough. Use steam," she said, and after giving me some medicine for her and nailing the dreaded red-and-white quarantine sign to the side of the house, she was off in a cloud of snow.

To add to our misery, the other boys came down with whooping cough, too. After a week of sleepless nights and crying kids, I thought things couldn't get much worse, but they did. Whooping cough was probably the only childhood disease I hadn't been exposed to, and I came down with it, too. In a household with no running water, no central heating, and very little room to move around, just getting through the day was a major challenge.

We had an old gas-powered washing machine with rubber rollers and a stove for heating the wash water in the old bunkhouse. With the abundance of snow that winter, we were spared having to haul all our water from the well in the pasture. There was always a boiler full of melting snow on the stove, and we had frozen clothes hanging on the line outside and in the upstairs room. Even with plenty of hot water it was next to impossible to keep clean dry clothes and bedding for all of us. "Mommy, I'm going to be sick," was the constant cry.

I was just fixing a steam tent for the baby when there was a loud knock on the back door. It was our carpenter. When I showed him the quarantine sign, he said he'd had scarlet fever and whooping cough, and he planned to stay until the "yob" was done.

Berge would have been a tall man if he had straightened up, but his back was permanently bent, probably from the years of leaning over a saw. If he ever smiled, I never caught him at it. He had arthritis in his knees, and every morning as he was combing his pale hair he would snarl "son-of-a-bitchin' knees," and glare at each of us as though we were somehow to blame. He fixed himself a pallet in the new addition, asked us if we knew how to play whist, and settled down for the duration. Ricky was cajoled into learning the game, and we wore out a whole box of mantles on the gas lamp that long winter.

There was constant war between Craig and Berge. Our carpenter's language was liberally sprinkled with salty phrases, and he called upon a higher power with every other sentence. In addition to a new vocabulary, Craig managed to pick up a hammer, nails, screws, and even Berge's box of snuff. Cries of "Where in the hell is that kid now?" rang in our ears. Several times a day Berge would grab Craig by the seat of his pants and empty out his pockets, cussing a sulfurous streak all the while. Those words were just a part of his everyday language, and he couldn't seem to express himself without them. Sawdust was everywhere, and the sound of the hammering, sawing, and crying kids was our background music.

The whooping cough wore on. Ricky continued to improve, but the coughing and sleepless nights were beginning to take their toll. The only way I could sleep at all was sitting up in the rocking chair, usually with one of the little ones on my lap. When spring finally arrived, we all recovered. The quarantine was lifted, and Alton and I went to town to pick out our new cupboards. It was heaven, getting out of the house at last—heaven just to be without little kids for a single afternoon.

There was a record amount of rain that summer, and I enthusiastically planted a huge garden, forgetting, as gardeners do, that harvesting follows planting. I picked, snapped, shelled, shucked, and canned day after day that fall. Once, after several days of canning, I looked at three big milk buckets of peas and thought of a plan that could cut my work in half. The old washing machine, which had served us so well, could be turned into a handy dandy pea sheller. Why hadn't I thought of this before?

I started the engine, picked up a handful of peas and fed them into the rollers. Green mush! I was sure I could get it to work if I just kept trying, so I loosened the rollers some more and started over. Soon I had peas in my hair, peas on the floor, and peas on the ceiling. The rollers were dyed a deep green, and I never did get the color out, although I used Clorox and Comet cleaner and lots of elbow grease. By the time I got things reasonably cleaned up, I could have shelled and canned six buckets of peas. I noticed Alton looking at the green rollers the next time he helped me with the wash, but he didn't ask, and I didn't volunteer any information.

Smoke Rings

It was one of those beautiful June days when everything seemed perfect. It looked like we'd have a crop, barring grasshoppers, hail, or fifty-mile-an-hour winds. Alton was working up in the "hidden field" and planned to work until dark. The little boys were playing by the barn when I went to check on them. Baby Sandra was sleeping, and there was nothing to worry about.

I watched the boys as they chased each other and thought how much alike they were, and yet, how different. Craig was born a year and eleven days before Alan and was always full of energy and curiosity. Alan was more deliberate and thoughtful. When he started to talk, Craig, the impatient one, would finish his sentences.

They were always together, so when we called them we would yell "Craig 'n Alan," and Craig would say, "Nalen he say he wanna drink." And Alan would say, "Yuh, yuh."

We always had a small flock of chickens, much to Craig's delight. Craig loved the chickens, and from the time they were newly hatched until their egg laying days, he could often be found playing with them. It was not unusual to see him walking around with a sleeping chicken tucked under his arm. Our rooster, though, was the meanest rooster I have ever seen. We always had to watch out for him and hope to outrun him when we were aiming for the backhouse, but there he'd be, neck and wings outstretched and blood in his eye.

One hot summer day I noticed the washtub out by the chicken coop where it shouldn't be and decided to investigate. I could see it moving and heard a faint crowing sound. When I reached for the tub, Alan and Craig came yelling. "Don't let him out—don't let him out! We put him in jail for beatin' up on those poor old hens!"

When I tipped the tub over, the rooster staggered off in the direction of the henhouse, tail feathers wet and dragging and comb crumpled in defeat. That night Alton and I had a talk, and Alton agreed that it was time to explain "Nature's Plan" to two little boys.

The old kitchen lean-to had been dragged away from the house and converted to a bunkhouse, and Alton's brother, Delos, stayed there when he came to help us out. We knew he was careless with cigarettes and matches, and it worried us a lot. The day Alton came home with a shiny red fire extinguisher I breathed a sigh of relief.

I had a timer that I would set for fifteen minutes, and I would check on the boys when it rang. One day I looked out the window and didn't see them, but I could hear them giggling so decided to get to my ironing. My basket of clothes was almost finished, and I was thinking about making an apple pie for supper when the boys ran in, slamming the door in their haste. Alan was doing the talking this time, so I knew something really serious was going on. "We got a fire in the bunkhouse!" He looked pretty scared, but Craig was right behind him. "No, it's ok, it's ok. It's only a little fire," he said. I grabbed the extinguisher and raced across the yard. Craig was right. It was only a little fire, about the size of a pie plate, and right in the middle of the bed.

I was just reaching for the screen door with the extinguisher at the ready when, Zing! Pop! Zing! Bullets started exploding in every direction. I grabbed the boys and ran to get out of range of those flying bullets. Had we been a few minutes earlier we would have been in there when they started exploding. I never felt so helpless in my life as I stood there shaking and hugging the boys. I could almost see the headlines. "Mad housewife shoots self and sons in blazing inferno! Police search for mystery weapon."

The fire was soon out of control, and there was nothing to do but watch as the flames crept up the wall of the old garage next to the bunkhouse. Alton hadn't seen the smoke from the hidden field, but all the neighbors were at our farm manning a bucket brigade when he drove into the yard. It was too late, though, and

I will never forget the excited but terrified look on those little boys' faces, the firelight shining in their eyes. Were we raising a couple of pyromaniacs? They steadfastly declared that they didn't know how the fire started, and nothing we could say would change their story.

Sunday morning the boys jumped into bed with Alton for their usual morning romp and were snuggled up one on each arm. "Where did you guys get the matches?" their dad asked. The load of guilt must have been too heavy, and they both started talking at once. They had found the matches in the pocket of Delos's overalls that were hanging on the wall. The twenty-two shells had fallen out of the pockets.

They shamefacedly admitted that they had been looking at the women's underwear in the Sears Roebuck catalog, and when they came to a particularly well-endowed model they would giggle over it and then crumple up the page and set it on fire. Apparently, they found a lot of them because their fire had a good start. At first they had tried to put it out by dumping dirt on it, but still the fire burned on.

This was big stuff, and Alton was in charge this time. They would have to be punished, not only for the fire, but also for lying about it. Alton would rather take a licking himself than hurt one of his kids, but this time he knew it had to be done. He usually gave them a choice, though, knowing that they would choose to give up a privilege rather than endure physical punishment. They knew in their hearts that the old, "This hurts me more than it does you," was really true. He hated having to punish them far worse than they hated being punished.

Windy Days

Wind was a constant on the farm. Dust would pile up on the windowsills and get in our teeth and the corners of our eyes. There were days when we could barely see the outline of the barn, and the sky was a sickly yellow. Sometimes the sun would shine like a blessing, and the rain would come just when we needed it. Then there were winds that caught the tumbleweeds and drove them into drifts in the corner fences, piled them high against the barn, and tore the clothes from the line to send them sailing across the pasture.

Occasionally Alton would take Craig and Alan along to the field with him when the weather was nice so I could have some time alone with baby Sandra. The little boys were four and five then, and he let them play nearby where he could keep an eye on them. This time they were playing by the remains of an old shack on a hill next to the field where Alton and Ricky were summer fallowing. He was scanning the sky, hoping the clouds were going to bring rain, when he saw the boys running down the hill toward him, waving and yelling, "We caught him, we caught him!" When he climbed down from the tractor and got closer, he could see that they were carrying an old lunch pail between them. He smelled the boys long before he reached them, and he had no doubt about what they had caught. They stank of skunk.

"Open the box, Daddy," they yelled. "Can we keep him?" When the latch was released, the baby skunk ran for a patch of thistles and disappeared.

"You guys are really going to catch it from your mom when you get home," Alton said. "Now get on up the hill and wait in the back of the pickup until Ricky comes to get you."

I had just put Sandra down for a nap and was scrubbing the kitchen floor when I saw them coming up the road. The house smelled of freshly baked bread and soap and clean clothes just brought in from the line. I had a pot roast in the oven and was feeling pretty pleased with my day when the door opened and those two sorry-looking kids stood there hanging their heads. Needless to say, the house no longer contained the fragrance of fresh bread, and it was days before it returned to normal. Although I washed and re-washed their hair and scrubbed them repeatedly, the smell remained with us. They ate their supper on the back porch that night, standing up. I buried their clothes, tennis shoes and all, someplace in the vicinity of the barn, I guess. I never did find them. I'm sure they're still entombed there, a sort of memorial to the family homestead.

Later I told the story to my friend, the editor of the *Hi-Line Herald*, and she printed it in the paper under the title "Skunk for Lunch?" Alton wasn't happy about having his name in the local paper, but news was scarce in those prairie towns, and it provided some laughs at a time when there wasn't much to laugh about, with the topsoil being blown away by the ceaseless wind.

Another windy day I was folding the wash when I saw the pickup go slowly past the kitchen window, headed for the windmill. I knew it was windy, but not windy enough to move the truck. I ran out waving my arms and yelling, but the pickup stopped just as I caught up with it. When I opened the door, Craig was on his knees steering, and Alan was on the floor, pushing the gas peddle. Just another normal day on the homestead.

More than once those days came close to ending in tragedy. Ricky was staying overnight with a friend, and I thought the other three were down for their naps, but when I went upstairs to check on them, Craig was missing. I searched everyplace for him, calling his name. He came around the corner of the granary staggering, and there was something blue around his mouth. I grabbed him and ran to the house, broke an egg, and forced him to swallow it. He gagged and threw up and then I had him drink two glasses of milk.

I could see Alton in the nearest field and ran out, waving a dish towel. He saw me and came at a dead run. Craig was still vomiting when we got Sandra and Alan up from their naps and hurried to the car, only to find that a rear tire was flat. We didn't have a spare. This was wartime, and tires were scarce. By the time we got the tire patched and drove to Havre, forty-five miles away, Craig was sleeping. The doctor said he couldn't have done much more for him than I already had.

It turned out Craig had eaten some blue vitriol that had blown down from the rafters of the granary. Blue vitriol was a substance for treating horses' hooves and had been stored up in the rafters twenty years or more ago. Craig had discovered the grain door, just big enough for him to crawl through, though why he put the blue vitriol in his mouth we never learned. He was bright-eyed and chipper the next morning, so he must not have swallowed much of it.

The closest we came to losing Craig was another windy day. Alton had built a cab for the tractor to protect the driver against the sun and wind and had fastened a screen door on the back to keep the flies and mosquitoes out. He had a tight spring latch on it, and just to be sure, a hook that he always kept fastened.

He was discing that day near the house, and Craig begged to go along for a ride. The vibrations had put him to sleep, and when Alton heard the screen door slam, he instantly pulled the clutch and hit the brakes. This time he had forgotten to latch the door, and Craig had fallen and was lying with his back right up against those sharp-as-knives discs, still asleep and unhurt. I saw Alton coming across the field carrying Craig and started praying. When he brought that sleeping little boy into the house the tears were streaming down his face, and he was as white as paper. He just sat down in the rocking chair with Craig in his arms and cried.

Years later, when I told that story at a family gathering, Alton got up from the table with tears in his eyes to give Craig, by then a grown man, a long hug.

Runaways

School would be out before long, and the kids had different opinions about summer vacation. Craig would miss his friends, and Ricky wasn't welcoming the long days on the tractor. Alan and Craig would be seven and eight in August, just old enough to be a worry but not big enough to be a help. I relied on the timer when they were out of my sight, but they still got into plenty of trouble.

One Saturday we gave the kids permission to have a picnic in O'Brien coulee, about a mile away. I was nervous at having them out of sight so long, with good reason as it turned out. Sandra was with them that time, but they promised to take good care of her. They came back earlier than I expected and seemed awfully subdued. One of them would run out to the barn every hour or so, and then they would have a whispered conversation. I knew they were up to something, but decided to wait it out.

The next day on my way to the garden I saw a strange animal hopping and floundering down toward the pasture. It looked about the size of a rabbit, but as I got closer it didn't look like any rabbit I had ever seen. Then I could see that it was a huge baby bird. It glared at me with its red-rimmed yellow eyes and opened its beak and hissed. It was such an ugly thing that I felt sorry for it. I left it there and ran back to the house in search of the boys. They had been watching me out the window and were ready with a story.

"It was all alone down in the pasture," they said, "and we brought it home to take care of it." They both had their sleeves rolled down and buttoned, which was unusual. I pulled Alan's sleeve up, although he protested, and there were deep scratches on his arms. They both had scratches on their hands and arms and had made a pact not to tell me, but when I saw the nasty looking wounds I kept at them until they told me what really happened. They had robbed an eagle's nest, fighting the mother bird as they climbed up the cliff. I'm not sure if it was an illegal act at that time, but I know it is now. Alton took the kids and the bird back to its nest and got a few scratches himself before he could finish his mission of mercy.

Shortly after that we had had a visit from the principal. "Is Alton around?" he asked. I knew there had to be a problem for him to drive out while school was in session. He didn't tell me what the trouble was, but they had a short conversation and then Alton took the pickup and followed him, heading for town. About an hour later he came back with a red-faced Craig and told him to go upstairs and wait for him. Then he lifted a sack full of something out of the back of the pickup and came in wearing a big grin.

"Are you going to tell me what's going on or not?" I demanded.

"Well, yes," Alton said. "The postmaster saw two little boys pulling a wagon along the highway and called the principal."

The other boy's parents were the cook and custodian of the school, and the culprits were nearly four miles up the road toward Gildford when they caught up with them. Craig was the ringleader, of course. He had had to talk fast to get Freddy to leave with him, especially after Craig took him up to the school one last time. "Say goodbye to your mother, Freddy, because you'll probably never see her again," Craig said. Freddy began to cry and had been about to mutiny, but when Craig reminded him of their plans to go to California where oranges hung from every tree, Freddy began to warm up to the idea again. They would swim in the ocean, Craig said, and lie in the sun that shone all year, and there wouldn't be any teachers to boss them around, or moms or big brothers and no school. Freddy reluctantly agreed.

They took a sack of potatoes, a side of bacon, a knife, matches, even a frying pan, and packed it all neatly in the wagon. They figured they were well supplied with all the necessities of life when they set off. They never did say why they were leaving home, and Craig declares to this day that he can't remember any reason why they left, except for the adventure. They had to give up a couple of recesses as punishment, but soon summer was upon us, and they were involved in other escapades.

The summers were full of danger for little kids on the farm. There were the trucks roaring through the yard, the combine and other machinery to fall from, the barn loft to climb in. Everyone knew about the child who had lost a foot in the grain auger. Like my mother, I always had a bottle of Lysol in the cupboard, and they never got infection from their cuts and bruises.

They worked for weeks one summer digging a hole that they intended to turn into a swimming pool, enlisting all their friends. Everyone dug, imagining the long cool afternoons swimming in the pool. Alton never said a word, but he was betting that they would get tired of it and move on to something else. When it was almost time for harvest and the grain trucks would be driving through, he had to intervene. "Hey, you guys," he said. "Have you thought about where you're going to get the water to fill that swimming pool?" By this time we had running water in the house, but we were still hauling all of our water from town to fill the cistern. The kids looked at each other and their faces fell. I felt almost as bad as they did when the neighbor came with his backhoe to push the dirt back into the hole and pack it down for the trucks.

"Why didn't you stop them sooner?" I asked. "It was cruel, letting them get their hopes up when you knew it was just a fantasy!"

"Several reasons," he said. "It kept them out of mischief all summer, they developed their muscles, and it taught them to think things through before tackling a project. That's the way life is."

Alton always gave the kids an allowance, but he did it differently than most dads. When harvest was over he gave each of them a check for their summer wages. I'm not sure how much it was, but Rick would cash his check and give me his money to put away. He always planned a ski trip with his friends in February and wanted to be sure he still had the money to pay for it when the time came.

"Now, Mom," he'd say, "don't give me more than five dollars a week, no matter how much I beg." It was hard to resist his pleading, but I managed to hold out until the ski trip was over each year. Alan would cash his check and put it with the money he still had from last year. Craig would spend all of his.

One year Craig decided that since his wages were so soon spent he would go into business. It was probably the merchant gene passed down from generations of storekeepers. He found a *Grit* magazine with an ad. "Double your income!" it said. "Sell *Grit*!" This was just what he was looking for, and he signed on the dotted line. He would be their representative.

I get a headache when I think of that winter. The big roll of papers would come in the mail. Sometimes they were undamaged, but more often they were wet or torn and his customers would complain, so he'd give them their money back and end up owing *Grit* money by the end of the month instead of the other way around. His bookkeeping left something to be desired, and I felt so sorry for him. I wanted just to give him the money and cross it off as a learning experience. "No," Alton said. "How is he going to learn a lesson if he doesn't have to face the consequences?" He was right, of course. I think Craig had to borrow from Alan against his next summer's wages before he and *Grit* parted company.

That wasn't the end of Craig as entrepreneur. One day while lining the garbage can with old copies of *Grit*, he found an ad that caught his eye. "START YOUR OWN BUSINESS! THOUSANDS ARE BEING MADE! START YOUR NUTRIA FARM TODAY! WRITE FOR DETAILS!"

I have to admit that I encouraged him when he showed the ad to me. He was so eager and optimistic, and it did make sense. I had seen a nutria coat in the Buttreys dress shop, and it was beautiful. A nutria is an animal about the size of a prairie dog, and its pelt is a lovely golden tan and very thick. The boys would have all the space they needed for their nutria ranch, and we would make cages as they reproduced. Nutria were more prolific than minks, the ad said. For a small down payment the nutria ranchers would receive a healthy pair—in separate cages, of course. "Otherwise," the ad said, "you would have a dozen or more nutrias by the time they arrived." The only hitch was that Craig had already spent his wages. He would have to find a venture capitalist.

Alan saw the gleam in his brother's eyes. "This doesn't look good to me," he said. "Count me out."

It took a week to convince him, but finally he decided he would do it if Dad thought it was a good idea. Alton solemnly went through all the pros and cons with them, and after he made them consider a long list of things that could go wrong, he gave them his blessing. Alan's stash was considerably smaller when the money was sent, and they settled down to wait. It was a long summer, with no furry little animals in sight. We envisioned hundreds of baby nutrias scampering through the railway cars, and although we wrote and finally tried to telephone the number we'd been given, all the boys received from the "company" was a letter saying a pair of healthy nutria had been sent to Alan and Craig Sterry at this address.

It was another lesson for Craig, dampening his enthusiasm for a business of his own and proving to Alan that some great philosopher was right. "Neither a borrower nor a lender be." And some smart fellow added, "Especially with a relative."

April Fool

All the car factories converted to tank production during World War II, and it was 1946 before new cars at last began rolling off the assembly line. Alton had to put down a substantial payment to get his name on a list before we could even be considered for a car. It would be our first new car, a Ford, of course. Alton was loyal to the company that made the Model T, our first courting car, which his dad had bought for him in Great Falls for the grand sum of fifty dollars.

We waited a long time, but finally the letter came, telling us that the car was in Seattle. I had hoped to go along and make a special trip out of it, but Maggie, our trusty babysitter, was on a trip of her own, so Alton decided to take the train to Seattle and drive it back by himself. Since the train no longer stopped at the little Hi-Line towns, we had to drive to Havre, forty-five miles away. I planned to stay at Alton's sister's place that night and drive home in the morning. The kids were excited about seeing their dad off on the train, and it was late as usual, so they were asleep by the time I got them back to Bernice's place. When I opened the back door Craig slid out before I could catch him and gashed his head on the curb. "Keep an eye on Craig, and try not to let him get in any more scrapes," was the last thing Alton had said to me. Here he'd barely gotten out of town before Craig was in trouble. Our little accident-prone kid had more than his share of bumps and bruises, but this was serious. He was bleeding a lot, so Bernice called the doctor and he came right out.

The doctor was a rotund little man with a big ego and a much younger wife, and he was annoyed at being called out after hours. He cleaned and taped the wound and then proceeded to give Craig a thorough examination. He pulled up his shirt and did a double take.

"What in God's name is this?" he said. "They look like tooth marks."

"They are tooth marks," I said.

He glared at me.

"He got into the pen with the mother pig last week, and she bit him before I could get him out."

He just shook his head. Then he noticed the cut on Craig's finger and his broken toe. "Don't you ever watch your children, Madam?"

It was late, I was tired and scared, and I didn't like his tone of voice. "Doctor," I said, "If you spent just half the time chasing after this little guy as I do, you wouldn't have so much weight to carry around."

One thing I knew for sure: I'd better not call on that doctor again if I needed one in a hurry.

Spring was in the air. You could smell it, feel it, and taste it. We sat at the kitchen table each night and studied the seed catalogues by lamplight. We made out our order for seeds and then sent for a hundred baby chicks. Alton set up an oil heater for keeping them warm while they grew from tiny balls of yellow feathers to succulent fryers in July. It wasn't easy. They required constant attention or they would turn into cannibals and begin pecking each other, or they would pile up in corners and smother the unlucky chicks at the bottom of the pile. When the heating system broke down there was nothing to do but bring them into the house. We had linoleum on all the floors then, so we made cardboard barriers and penned them up in the living room.

Wouldn't you know the minister chose that night to come visiting with his family? Try having a meaningful conversation with a man of God in a small room with ninety or so peeping chicks, especially when he says, "Let us kneel and pray."

We got through the evening, blew out the lamps, and eventually the chicks quieted down, except for one little chick. You can't believe how loud one little peep-peep-peep can be when you're trying to sleep. I heard the door to the boy's bedroom open and shut, the sound of running feet on the stairs, the front door open and slam shut, and then blessed quiet. I knew for a certainty that there would be one less chicken in the pan next harvest. Rick came down to breakfast the next morning, red-eyed and ready for a confrontation, and when nobody said a word he announced stonily that he would never eat chicken again in his entire life.

I was just turning the calendar over to April when the kids came giggling down to breakfast. They had a great plan for an April Fool's joke on their dad, and I went right along with it. Alan and Craig went outside and then slammed the door on their way in. "Dad! Dad! The heater's off in the brooder house," they yelled.

Alton came tearing out of the bedroom, wild-eyed, red hair on end, hopping on one foot and trying to get the other in his pant leg. When we all yelled "April Fool," I thought he would explode. He did have a sense of humor, but it was a bit too much for him to find the humor in this. He was pretty sharp with us the rest of the day. We all hung our heads, and it sort of took the fun out of April Fool's Day for a while, but the memory of him hopping on one foot with his hair sticking out all over still makes me laugh.

I never quite gave up on April Fool's Day, though. Sandra tells me that every year, when April 1 approaches, she loses her car keys, forgets to set the alarm, or has a bad hair day—all as a result of being traumatized by one of my April surprises when she was a child. The worst one was when I baked a batch of cupcakes and decorated them for her to take to school as a treat for her class. She was in the third grade and happy to be able to impress her teacher. The trouble was, the cupcakes had all been baked with a cotton ball in the middle. And her teacher did not have much of a sense of humor. Fortunately Sandra did.

Sandra was a quiet, thoughtful child, an Amdahl for sure. She watched and remembered. She has related, in the smallest detail, incidents that I can barely recall. She would make up her mind to do something, and nothing could stop her. For instance, there was the ongoing great taffy feud. Almost every time Alton and I went someplace for the evening Sandra would drag out the pans and start a batch of taffy. To my knowledge, it never turned out, and we knew the minute we came in the door that she had made another attempt. She always made an effort to clean up after herself, but there would be residue of taffy on the door handles, the stove, even the mop handle. My memory is sketchy on this, but according to Sandra, I came roaring up the stairs one time and jerked her out of bed, marched her down to the kitchen, and made her cut the taffy recipes out of all the cookbooks and burn them in the sink.

We had our share of mother-daughter clashes, and I can't help smiling to myself these days as rampant hormones beset her own daughter.

The Red Hat

The long war was over and ration books would soon be a thing of the past. Industry was tooling up for postwar America. Farmers who had kept their machinery running with spit and baling wire were finally able to buy new implements, making the backbreaking, dawn-to-dark days a little easier. Sandra was born that year, the crops were abundant, the price of wheat was up, and life was good.

Alton gave me my own checkbook, and although I knew there would be a day of reckoning, I sometimes got a little carried away. Hats were my downfall. We wore hats then, and gloves, to church, to P.T.A., and even shopping. And I had found the perfect hat—the hat of the century! It was a deep ruby red with a sweeping brim, and it had a purse to match. I knew it was far beyond my means, but there was always the hope that it would go on sale.

When we made our infrequent trips to Havre, I would visit THE HAT. When I lifted it down from its velvet stand and settled it on my head, I became a woman to be reckoned with, a woman of style and glamour, and three inches taller. It was a glorious hat—a hat with verve and passion—a hat to shrivel the hearts of every other woman in the county with envy.

It was customary for the wives to gather at the Elks Club after a session of shopping. We could bring our children for a "Shirley Temple" as we waited for happy hour with our husbands. One dismal day in January my life was brightened when I hurried to the shop to check on my hat, as I was beginning to call it. Was I mistaken or was that a sale ticket attached to the brim? My heart beat a little faster as I took it down. "I'll take it," I said, without even looking at the reduced price.

"You don't know how lucky you are," the sales clerk said. "Another woman has been coming in every week, and she really wanted it badly. I expected her in today, in fact, and I just finished marking it down as you came in the door. Wear it in good health," she chirped.

It was an omen, I thought. The hat was surely meant for me, but I winced as I peeked at the sale ticket. Ten dollars! Far too much for something I didn't need. Alton would give me a lecture over this, I knew.

Filled with the elation that only a successful shopping trip can bring, I carried my trophy to the Elks Club. There, sitting at the bar, was the only woman I have ever been jealous of. Jean was a teacher in our school with her own private income and the wife of Alton's best friend, George. She had a magnificent bosom, luxuriant auburn hair, and was taller than I. She beckoned me over, her smile thinning as she noticed the big sack with Lamode emblazoned on it.

"Alton's going to kill me," I whispered. "I've just spent ten dollars for a hat."

"If it's the hat I'm thinking of," she said, "I'm going to kill you first."

Then, pulling the sack from my limp hands, her eyes narrowed. She peeked inside.

"It . . . It is . . . My hat!"

"It isn't your hat," I said. "I bought it and I'm going to keep it and wear it to . . . to the Mother's Day breakfast at the Elks Club."

"Do you plan to tell Alton how much you spent?" she said. "Go ahead, put it on, and you'll see that it just isn't right for you. The brim is too wide. It isn't your color. And you're too short to wear a hat like that."

I was beginning to weaken, and she went for the jugular. " I'll give you five dollars more than you paid for it." Then, pressing her advantage, she said, "Why don't we both model it and let the others decide?" She really wanted that hat.

I flinched as she put the hat on my head. "Walk," she said.

I walked, getting shorter by the minute, as some of my friends gave me lukewarm applause. Then, placing the hat on her auburn hair, and looking like the *Queen Mary* leaving the harbor, she did a slow "Mae West" twice around the room, accompanied by whistles and cheers from the men.

I knew it would never again really be my hat. "Alright," I said, "take it!"

She had her purse open and the money in my hands quicker than a snake and was still wearing that beautiful hat when Alton walked in. The first thing he said was "Where did you get that hat, Jean? You look like a million dollars!" Then, turning to me, he said, "Why don't you ever wear hats like that, honey?"

The Accident

T he August of 1956 was the only time in my memory that we were ready for harvest before it was ready for us. The machinery was repaired, the trucks gassed up and ready to go, and the freezer was full of chicken and homemade buns.

"We have at least three days before the wheat is ripe," Alton said to Craig and Alan, "and we can get most of the rock picked before you guys have to go back to school."

This time I objected. "We're all tired, Alton. Couldn't we just this once give the kids some vacation time before school starts? Can't the rocks wait a week or two?" He reluctantly agreed, and I made reservations at the Elk Park Resort in Canada, north of Havre and just across the Canadian border.

Rick had graduated from high school the previous spring and had spent the summer working on the town's new sewer system. It was the first time Rick had ever worked for anyone except his dad, and he was enjoying his independence. He had other plans for the weekend, he said, so we left without him.

Ray and Ilse, the Hingham school superintendent and his wife, decided to join us. Those cabins were primitive at best, and none too clean, so Ilse and I spent a couple of hours with a bucket of soapy water and scrub brushes before we unpacked. The cabins were made of logs, and we could see daylight where the plaster had fallen out. In fact, they were about the size of the teacherages I had grown up in, with a makeshift closet and open shelves over the sink. I don't know why I thought this was going to be a vacation. The stove was an old iron range, used mainly to take the chill off in the mornings.

Alton really needed to unwind and spent most of the first two days sleeping. The kids rented a boat and caught a nice bunch of fish for supper. Craig would be thirteen in a few days, and he and Alan were excited about driving the grain trucks that year. That had been Ricky's job, but Ricky was leaving Montana to attend college in California. I think more than anything it was to get as far away from the farm as possible. When Ricky left for California he said he was never coming back to work on the farm, and he never did.

Once he had enough rest, Alton began getting nervous, sure that we would return home to find all the neighbors in the harvest field ahead of him. "It's time to go back," he said on the afternoon of the second day. We all pleaded with him to at least wait until the next morning, and he gave in, so we packed up and went to bed early.

I was troubled by a series of dreams that night about Alton's dad. I dreamed I saw him dancing in a green meadow in a circle of strangely familiar people, all of them dressed in long white tunics. It was so unsettling that I couldn't go back to sleep. I saw by my watch that it was four, and it was just starting to get light out, so I got up and gathered some woodchips to start the fire. Ilse came out on the steps in her robe and beckoned to me. She had an electric coffeepot and brought a cup for each of us. We sat down at the picnic table, and I couldn't get that strange dream out of mind, so I told her about it. She said she, too, had been having upsetting dreams.

The sky was overcast that morning, and a strong wind was blowing, washing the waves high on the shore of the lake, whipping the trees and bringing the strong smell of cedar and wood smoke. We watched the clouds pile up as we got the family fed and ready to start home. Ilse and Ray decided to stay one more night, but we weren't too sorry to be leaving. The holiday spirit had evaporated, and we were pretty quiet on the drive back to Havre.

The immigration checkpoint was in the Havre courthouse, and Alton drove straight there. "Wait in the car," he said. "This will only take a minute." When he came out, his face was ashen. "Pa is dead," he said. "There was an accident, and Ma is in the hospital in serious condition."

Rick was sitting beside Maggie's bed when we arrived at the hospital, and he broke down and cried when we walked in. It was the first time he had been able to let go. He told us that he had just returned home from work when a car came tearing up the road. It was one of the Pester boys. "Your grandma and grandpa were in an awful accident," he told him. "The ambulance is on its way, but you need to be there." Rick grabbed his coat, and they took him to the scene of the accident, a mile east of our farm. He was in charge from then on.

Olaf had taken Maggie for a ride to see the wheat fields, which were beautiful that August evening. They were crossing the gravel road when a fuel truck came speeding over the blind hill. They never had a chance. The truck plowed into them, and Olaf was crushed. Rick held his grandpa's head while they waited for the ambulance and sat beside him in the ambulance until they reached the hospital in Havre.

Maggie's left leg, arm, hip, and shoulder were all broken, and she was put in a cast from shoulder to ankle, but she refused to take any pain medicine.

Alton's sister Margie and his brother Norman were already on their way from Seattle. The others were too stunned to make decisions, so Rick had made the phone calls. Delos, Alton's younger brother, was there with Rick, but he was too shocked to be of any help. After all the phone calls had been made, Rick and Delos got a hotel room but were wakened by a call. Olaf was sinking fast. They were at his bedside when he died at four in the morning, just when I was waking from my dream.

Rick was glad to turn things over to Alton, who took care of the funeral arrangements. He was the one to tell Maggie that her husband had died. I grieved for Alton's pain and because I hadn't been able to make it up to Ole for all the times I had given him trouble, but Sandra felt the loss more than the others. She was her grandpa's favorite in our family, and it took her a long time to get over his death.

Olaf was still the representative for McNess Company, a position he'd held for more than fifty years, and it seemed that everyone in Hill County was there for his funeral. The family never suspected that he had so many friends. Both the church and the basement were crowded with his old customers. People stood against the walls and gathered outside the church, and cars lined both sides of the street three blocks away.

When the family had gone back to their homes and harvest was in full swing, there was a feeling of normalcy again. Maggie hated the hospital and made plans to come to the farm in September, and there was no talking her out of it. We rented a hospital bed, a commode, and other essentials, and a month after the accident she was brought out to the farm by ambulance. I never saw her cry, although she was grieving deeply. The hardest thing for her was being dependent on me. Maggie was the most fiercely independent woman I have ever known beside my mother, and it was a clash of wills between us from the start.

She hated having to allow me to bathe and feed her. She hadn't been very gracious when I was a green, young bride, and she had to help me out. Now the tables were turned, and she resented it. She refused to use the commode and said she would use the bedpan until she could go to the bathroom by herself. She would feed herself, too, or she wouldn't eat, she said. It wasn't an easy task, getting her on the bedpan, and bathing her was very difficult. She weighed at least two hundred pounds and had since I first met her.

Maggie wanted a calendar to mark off the days, so I taped the pages to a cardboard backing and fastened a pencil to it with a piece of string. She promptly circled the days when she would get out of bed for the first time, when she would go to the bathroom by herself, and even the day she would take the train to North Dakota to see her sister. You have to respect determination like that.

The Spicher family had been the Sterrys' closest neighbor, having homesteaded about three miles away. One day George and Richard came out to visit Maggie and were shocked to see her in that body cast looking pale and wasted. George had tears in his eyes when they left. "I don't think she will ever get out of that bed, Sterry," he said.

Maggie fooled us all.

We set up a television in Maggie's room, and Oral Roberts was running Lawrence Welk a close second as her favorite T.V. show. When the reverend exhorted his viewers to reach out and touch a chair or other object while he said a healing prayer, she entered into it wholeheartedly. I can't explain it, but despite all her broken bones she reached every one of her goals, and right on time.

Alan was his grandma's good right hand. When he came in from the field he would see if there was anything she needed. He brought her popsicles from the freezer and made sure she had a glass of ice water at her bedside. No one ever had to ask him, he just knew what needed to be done.

"Grandma, why don't you teach Mom to bake some of your brown bread?" he asked one day. Nothing could have pleased Maggie more. The only trouble was that she guarded her recipe with her life, and she sure wasn't going to let me in on her secret. She solved the problem. "Just mix the sponge like you do for your own whole wheat bread, and then bring the bowl to me," she said. She would taste it. "Put in a little bitsa salt. Now a bitsa more sugar." Then molasses, then some grape nuts soaked in half cup of milk. For each baking she had me put something different in the dough—a little more of this, a little less of that. She was delighted to be in charge again. I never tried to make her bread without her help because it meant so much to her. And I never did get her recipe.

Several times a day she would ask one of the boys or Alton to help her stand up for a few minutes and eventually to help her walk a few steps. The day came when she was ready, she said, to go to the bathroom. I was against it, but finally gave in. "Just don't lock the door," I said. She had Alton and Craig help her up, and then she moved as fast as I had ever seen her. She was through the bathroom door with the latch turned before I could stop her. I could imagine her on the floor with more broken bones and yelled at her to unlock the door. I could just picture her smiling into the mirror. Privacy at last! She didn't answer and she didn't unlock the door until she was good and ready, and she never used the bedpan again.

She was doing so well that we thought it was time for her to have a wheelchair. "If you get one of those things you'll have to sit in it, because I won't," she said firmly.

I have to admit that although I had boundless respect for Maggie's courage, the winter months stretched ahead long and burdensome. I hadn't felt this shut in since Alan and Craig were babies. We couldn't leave Maggie alone, and I should have insisted that we get someone to stay with her once in a while so Alton and I could go someplace together. Failing that, I could have asked Alton to stay with his mother occasionally so I could get away. Instead I just let the frustration build. I wanted to get out of the house and go to a dance or a movie. One morning I exploded. Alton said he had to go to Havre for repairs, and, of course, I couldn't go along. "Why can't I go and get the repairs?" I asked. "I've done it many times before when you were too busy."

We argued, and it ended with me jumping in the car and just driving north, crying all the way. When I got home an hour later I found that Alton had taken the pickup and gone to Havre, leaving Maggie alone. I was furious, but she was smiling. "See," she said. "I told you I didn't need a babysitter."

The day we took Maggie to Havre and put her on the train for North Dakota was a triumph of determination. After the visit with her sister she went to Seattle and stayed through the winter, but on April 15 she boarded the train again and came to stay with us on the farm. That was to be the first of ten summers she spent with us. I can't say that she was any trouble. She did a lot of little chores around the house, peeling potatoes for supper, shelling peas, and folding clothes. She talked to the chickens while she was gathering eggs and seemed happy to be living at the farm where she had raised her family.

Maggie and I still had our clashes. She was walking without a noticeable limp by that second summer and often walked down to the pasture alone. Once she cut her leg crawling through a rusty barbed wire fence and didn't tell us about it. A couple of days after that she didn't come down to breakfast. It worried me because she was always up before anyone, sipping her boiled coffee and watching the sunrise. When I opened her bedroom door she was laying on her back. Her face was flushed and hot, and she was having difficulty breathing. She woke when I touched her and seemed disoriented.

"What's the matter, Maggie?" I asked. "You look pretty sick to me."

"Nah, nah, nah, I just have a little bitsa cold."

"Can I bring you some coffee? Maybe that will help."

"If you would be so kind," she said.

I ran down to the kitchen and caught Alton just as he was going out the door to the field. "Your mother is sick, and she needs to see a doctor," I said.

"What makes you think she's sick? Just leave her alone," he told me. "She'll probably be all right. She hates doctors."

"Well, at least come up and look at her."

He followed me up, and I gave Maggie the coffee, which she drank and then promptly threw up.

"Ma, you really do look pretty sick," Alton said.

She glared at him. "Well, I'm not going to a doctor."

I pulled back the sheet that covered her legs and saw that there was a big black spot on her calf the size of a silver dollar with a red streak running up her leg.

"That looks like blood poisoning, Alton," I said. "She has to see a doctor."

"I'm not going," she said, and started to put on her clothes.

Alton looked at me and shrugged. "She won't go. What can I do?"

"Just go on downstairs so I can get dressed and clean up this mess," Maggie said.

I tried to help her get dressed but she would have none of it. It was a struggle, but she got her clothes on and came down the steps hanging onto the rail. She was gasping for breath as she made it to her chair.

"I'm staying right here," she said.

I went upstairs and came thumping down with my suitcase. "If you want to stay here and die of blood poisoning I can't stop you," I said. "But I won't be around to see it happen. I'm going to my sister's place in Cut Bank."

Poor Alton was standing there between two stubborn women, and he didn't know what to do with either of us.

"Oh, alright. I'll go stay with Bernice if I'm not welcome in your home," she said.

I packed some clothes for her, cleaned up the mess upstairs and we were on our way. When we arrived in Havre, Alton's sister Bernice took one look at her mother and called a doctor who put her in the hospital and kept her there for four days. Maggie was pretty cool with me when we brought her home. "They didn't do anything at that hospital that I couldn't have done myself," she grumped. "All I needed was a flaxseed poultice."

Surprise

After two years of Army service Rick was attending school at Northern Montana College in Havre. Craig was enrolled as a freshman there, and Alan, our farmer, was Alton's right-hand man. Sandra was a sophomore in high school, going steady with a basketball star from the nearest town. It looked like our family was about to leave the nest, and we could relax.

I had just turned forty that summer, and the family was nearly grown when I realized one day that I was all caught up. No bag of sprinkled clothes waiting for the iron, no jeans to be mended, all the socks matched and tidily in the dresser drawers.

I had been a reader all my life and secretly dreamed of someday being a writer, but there just hadn't been enough hours while the kids were young. What better time than now? Three friends and I decided to meet every two weeks to discuss our writing projects and learn from each other.

One day I heard about some Mexican sheepshearers expected soon at a ranch south of Gildford where I had stayed with Mama and worked one summer. I decided to write a story about them and see if I couldn't get it published. If I hadn't known the owner I probably wouldn't have been allowed at such a busy time, but when I called he agreed to let me visit, and I was up and on the road before daylight the next morning. I was delighted at the little tent village set up in the pasture. The mellow sound of Spanish blended with the bleating of the lambs staked outside the tents; the smell of the breakfast fires, along with the sound of a single guitar, set the stage for my story.

I worked almost as hard as the shearers did, taking several rolls of film, some of them from the barn roof. I drove to Havre and got the pictures developed and sent them to the editor of the *Great Falls Tribune*. I received a phone call within the week. They liked the story, they said, and since it was so timely, they would use it. It felt like Christmas and my birthday all rolled into one as I waited each Sunday for my story to appear.

Shearing season was long over and my enthusiasm considerably dampened by midsummer when I concluded that my story wasn't going to be printed after all. I had almost forgotten about it when I got a phone call the next April. It was the editor of the *Tribune* and he had called to tell me that they were going to run the story on the front page of the *Parade* section that very week. I was walking two feet off the ground when I received that Sunday paper and read my byline. I smiled for days. Maybe I could be a writer after all.

My sister Maribelle and her husband were coming for a visit, and I was in a flurry of baking and housecleaning. I blamed my hammering headaches on the excitement and stress, but Maribelle insisted that I ride as far as Great Falls with them when they left so that I could see my doctor there. Alton was to meet the bus in Havre that night when I returned, and the doctor agreed to get me right in when I got to the clinic.

After asking a few questions, and the usual poking and prodding, he gave me a strange look. "Let me see now," he said. "You're how old?"

"My age is right there in your records," I said testily. "I'm forty-three."

"Yes, well, are you driving your car today?"

When I told him that I was going back to Havre on the bus that afternoon, he asked me if I had someplace to stay till then. I was getting a little uneasy.

"Do you have some bad news for me? Is that what all these questions are about?" I demanded.

"That depends upon what you consider bad news," he said. Then, making a tent of his fingers, he looked at the ceiling. "You're about three months pregnant," he said. I must have turned white, because he asked again if I had someplace I could go. Right then

I couldn't have told him the names of my children, let alone of some nebulous friend in the city.

After the shock had worn off a little I remembered that one of Rick's friends was married and living in Great Falls. I called, and they said to come right over. The doctor gave me a tranquilizer and sent me off in a taxi. When Rick's friend and his wife saw how pale and shaky I was, they had me lie down, and I promptly fell asleep. They had to give me two cups of strong coffee to get me awake enough to get on the bus.

I had a lot of thinking to do on that long trip to Havre. How was I going to break the news to Alton? To say that I had mixed emotions was putting it mildly. On one hand, we had a chance to do it right this time. We could throw the old Doctor Spock books away and have fun with this child. On the other hand, I wouldn't have a full night's sleep for another two years! Nor did I relish being pregnant at the same time as the wives of some of Rick's friends. By the time I got to Havre, I had decided that despite future sleepless nights and diaper pails, I, at least, was going to enjoy this baby as I hadn't had time to enjoy the others.

When the bus pulled in at the station that evening my stomach clenched as I saw Alton waiting for me. He hugged me as he helped me down the steps. "Honey," he said, " I'm going to take you out for the biggest steak in Havre tonight."

I hugged him back. "Maybe you'd better wait and find out just what it is you're celebrating," I said.

He looked at me for a minute. "Is it twelve more years in P.T.A.?"

Now how could he have guessed when I hadn't had a clue? The same way he always knew the contents of his Christmas packages before he opened them, I suppose.

The day Jill was born I felt so good that when a few twinges started around noon I ignored them, but I did check to see if my suitcase was packed. Sandra called from school and said she had a headache and wanted Alton to come and get her. Our good friends, the Patricks, stopped in on their way to town to see how

I was getting along, and Craig drove in from Havre just as Alton came bringing Sandra home.

I put on a pot of coffee, never indicating that anything was happening, and when I lifted the coffee pot to pour, my water broke. Within minutes I started having hard labor. I grabbed a stack of towels, Alton took my suitcase, and we were off. The pains were three minutes apart, and we had forty-five miles to go.

We made it just in time. Alton sighed and lit a cigarette. "I suppose I'll have this whole pack smoked before it's over," he said to no one in particular. Before he finished the cigarette the nurse popped in. "You have a beautiful baby girl," she said.

Within two hours the room was full of grown people, all of them ours. Sandra's boyfriend brought her to the hospital, and Craig had turned around and driven right back to Havre, taking Alan with him. Rick came in with tears streaming down his cheeks. It was an emotional moment for all of us.

There were a lot of sleepless nights. Jill was subject to ear-aches, and we made many midnight calls to the doctor. His advice—give her a cool bath, give her an enema, give her a baby aspirin, and call me in the morning—wasn't much help. Sometimes we got back to sleep and sometimes we took turns sitting up with her until morning. It was all worth it though, and we enjoyed her as much as we thought we would.

When Jill was about six months old I found an ad in the *Ladies Home Journal* that promised any mother could teach her baby to read. The kit cost fifteen dollars, and when it arrived I saw that it contained flash cards, starting out with the first three alphabet letters. According to the instructions those three letters were the hardest part of the learning process. Once the child mastered them, the brochure said, the possibilities were endless. The lessons proceeded with words like "nose," "eyes," "hand," and finally to the words for the large objects in the room—stove, refrigerator, chair, and table. I was really having fun and was convinced that we were raising a genius.

Meanwhile, sixteen-year-old Sandra was discovering her own power as a woman. With our limited sleep we couldn't sit up and wait for her when she had dates, so we devised the perfect plan. We set the alarm clock to ring at 11:30 and put it beside our bed when she left. She'd better be there to turn it off before it reached the magic hour, we told her.

One of her hopefuls came early one night and, nervous at meeting the parents, he grabbed the first chair he came to and sat, hoping she would hurry. That chair happened to be in the kitchen. I saw him peering at first one and then the other labeled appliances. "Stove." "Refrigerator." "Sink."

"I suppose you're wondering what all of those signs are for," I said before I could stop myself. Just then Sandra entered the room, radiant and flashing her dimples. "Well, you see, we're trying to teach Sandra to cook."

She didn't have much interest in the boy, and he never showed up again, but I think I had just fired the first volley in the inevitable war between a teenage daughter and her mother.

Jill was the only one of the kids to grow up with television, and I confess I enjoyed the cartoons and *Play School* almost as much as she did. Her favorite shows were *Secret Squirrel* and *Galloping Granny*, and she even talked to the characters when the T.V. wasn't turned on. One morning when she was three, I was having a hard time getting her to put her clothes on. "I can't . . . I can't," she kept saying.

Finally, exasperated, I asked Alton to see if he could persuade her to get dressed. He asked her the question that hadn't occurred to me. "Why can't you?"

"Cause I can't get nekkid in front of my friends," she said.

"Alright, you guys," Alton said without a moment's hesitation, "follow me into the kitchen." In five minutes, she had her clothes on and was ready for the day. He knew just how her mind worked, and it was to be like that for the rest of their lives.

It seemed that the years between babyhood and kindergarten flew by. The speed at which she learned to talk and learned her alphabet, her fascination with books, and her ability to play by herself was almost magical. Jill was more like Alton than the rest of the family, and, like him, has always been a very private person. The year she was twelve I sent away for some garments that I thought she soon would need. When I gave them to her after school one night she just glared at me and grabbed the package out of my hand as she raced upstairs. Nothing more was said about the items, but one day I was looking for eggs when I saw something white sticking up through the straw in the chicken coop. When I pulled it out, the little bundle of bras told me plainer than words what she thought of my purchase.

When Jill was twelve she talked us into letting her bring a calico kitten home. We reminded her that calicos are always female, and she would have to get it spayed. She said she didn't care; she would pay for it herself. Time went on, and Clover grew into a cat sooner than we thought she would and presented us with six beautiful kittens. We were lucky and found homes for all of them. Then one day our neighbor phoned Jill to tell her that her kitty had another boyfriend. Jill phoned the veterinarian, and he said to bring the cat in and he would operate on her and spay her at the same time.

Jill and her best friend had earned quite a bit of money that summer babysitting. One day I happened to be just behind them as they walked down the street. "Look at the turquoise ring I got with my summer money," I heard Jill's friend say. "What did you get?" There was a long pause. "I didn't get anything," Jill said. "I had to spend my money for an abortion."

I was glad that I was the one behind them instead of the town gossip.

Easter Basket

April was always a fickle month. One week we would be standing in a snowdrift, and the sky would be cloudless, and the air would smell of spring. Our thoughts would turn to gardening, spring house-cleaning, and what we would wear for Easter Sunday. I would spend my spare time sewing a dress for Sandra and new shirts for the boys. There was such a feeling of renewal, of promise. We felt then that all our hopes and dreams were possible. But there was a dark side. Sometimes it seemed that trouble was in the very air we breathed in this pre-Easter season. Maybe it was because of the long cold, cheerless winter, but every year around this time meanness seemed to come out of the very woodwork. It was a time when old friendships were severed, when husbands didn't come home for supper, wives cried in their sleep, the milk curdled, and the bread wouldn't rise.

The trouble always started on Ash Wednesday when the Catholic kids came to school with a daub of ash on their foreheads. The teasing was merciless. The school became a war zone with "us" against "them."

It had been a hard winter, but Sandra hadn't noticed. She had been elected cheerleader and was going steady with a nice, good-looking boy from a nearby town. He was a basketball star, and his team was our archrival. Sandra was troubled with bouts of tonsillitis, and the doctor had advised against surgery. He thought she would grow out of it, but when she had secondary infections and was passing them on to Jill, he decided to remove Sandra's tonsils. She was dreading it. The operation turned out to be more difficult than we had thought it would be. She was pretty sick, so she had to stay in the hospital longer than we expected.

Her boyfriend brought her a dozen roses, which I thought was a bit much for a sixteen-year-old girl. After a few days' rest

at home she returned to school but came home that first afternoon looking dejected. She said none of the girls would speak to
her and wouldn't tell her why. This went on for a week, and then
another week, and now none of the kids would even sit with her
at lunchtime. She began to invent excuses for staying home, and
it was almost as hard on me as it was on her. I tried to talk to
Alton about it, but he was on the school board and didn't think
it was proper to get involved.

Things finally came to a head when the sophomore girls were
invited to the Havre Library for a tea. Sandra went to school that
day dressed up and ready to go with the rest of the girls. One of
them had her mother's car, and they just drove away without her.
Since this was a school function, I felt it was time to step in. It
seemed clear to me that one of the teachers should have been
with them. Alton still wouldn't do anything about the situation,
but I'd had enough.

I phoned the principal and told him I was coming in to see
him. When I confronted him he admitted that he knew what was
happening, and he didn't have a satisfactory explanation for letting it go on. He even knew which girls were responsible for
circulating stories about Sandra. He didn't know, or said he didn't
know, what the stories were. The next day the principal had
Sandra's classmates up before the assembly tearfully admitting
that they had lied. They were mad at Sandra for dating a mem-
ber of the rival basketball team and insisted she break up with
him, which she had refused to do. Some of the other girls came
to Sandra and suggested that they shun the two girls who had
started the whole thing. "I wouldn't want anyone to go through
what I just did," she said. "Let's forget it ever happened." I was
never prouder of her than I was that day.

Each year as Easter approached it seemed as though I would
never get all the projects done that I had started. Dyeing the eggs
after supper was just another chore, but the kids loved it. My
family was nearly grown before they got over the fun of hiding

Easter eggs. I would be working buttonholes or hemming a skirt or sewing in a zipper until midnight, doing a last-minute ironing or putting my hair up in curlers before I could get to sleep. I remember many times waking up with a jolt at three in the morning with a feeling of panic. What had I forgotten? The candy eggs. I had forgotten to hide the eggs!

They never did find all of them, even though I had been half asleep when I hid them. All spring we would find calcified candy eggs in light fixtures and tucked behind pictures. In August of 1996 we found some of those Easter eggs the day we burned the old house down. I suppose we could have dragged the house down to the pasture with the rest of the relics: the skeleton of our first truck, the stone boat, and the rusty twelve-foot plows. Sometimes I wish we had.

Alan was the only one still living at the farm at that time, and the old house had a leaky roof, worn out wiring, and rusty pipes that froze every winter. He decided to buy a new manufactured home. He placed his new house back closer to the windbreak. The kitchen in his new house was a dream, with enough cupboards to store a month's supply of groceries. There were two skylights, one in the master bathroom and the other in the big kitchen, and there were plenty of windows. I envied him. Comparing it to the old house before we had electricity was like comparing the old wringer washer to the shiny new washer and dryer in his tidy washroom.

The day we burned the old house was a day we will always remember. We all agreed that getting rid of it wouldn't make any difference in our lives. In fact, we would make a party out of the event and gather the clan for a final farewell. Allen Chinadle came over with his big bulldozer, and they had a water truck in case the fire somehow got away. We watched as the big machine took huge bites from the corners of the house and pushed the rest into the old basement, all except the brick chimney. It wouldn't fall, and I imagined little ghosts bracing against the sides, refusing to let it give in. I saw Alton's face as the pile of rubble was torched and knew the pain he must be feeling. He had worked so hard to make it into a home for us. There was the space he and I shared for nearly fifty years. The "dinosaur" was chewing it up, and I could feel Alton's heart breaking. It had turned cold, and I grabbed a coat from the rack and took it out to him.

"Let's sit in the pickup." He opened the door and helped me in. "It's tougher than I thought it would be," he said, trying to grin, but it was more of a grimace. He reached over and squeezed my hand, and there were tears in his eyes. Alton was a stoic, and it was a rare moment when he showed his feelings.

The heat from the fire was tremendous. We had to back the pickup away, and Alan trained the water hose on the near side of his new house. Smoke filled the air long after the fire had died to a smolder, and we had to keep Alan's air conditioner going in the house in order to breathe in there. I couldn't go to sleep that night, but lay awake watching the tongues of red and green flame lick around the remnants of the chimney.

Sandra, Alton, and I drove back to Flathead Lake, where Alton and I were living, the next day. That was the last time Sandra saw her dad. It was one of the best visits they'd ever had together. It was a beautiful drive along the edge of Glacier Park. The fall colors glowed in the afternoon sun as we listened to Nat King Cole all the way home.

Dark Times

There are dark times in everyone's life, and I wouldn't be honest if I didn't include some mention of mine. Jill was just learning to walk when I had the heart attack. I had felt nauseated most of the night, and didn't feel like going to church, so I stayed home with Jill. By the time the family returned I was feeling a little better and decided to go to my writer's meeting that afternoon. Norma Bangs picked me up, and we were halfway to Mary Welte's place when I suddenly felt a jolt just under my left arm that took my breath away. Gasping with pain, I broke out in a cold sweat that soaked my dress. I could barely breathe by the time we arrived at Mary's place. She had me lie down and checked my pulse. Mary had taught first aid, and she could see that my color wasn't improving, so she phoned Alton and told him her husband was bringing me home. Rick happened to be visiting and took me to the hospital in Chester where we found that the doctor was hoeing in the hospital garden five miles away.

When the wave of pain started again, Rick yelled at the nurses until they put me on oxygen while he went to get the doctor, who informed me that I had experienced a myocardial infarction. I was in the hospital for two weeks, and the neighbors helped in so many ways. Rose Farnik, the mother of four boys, took Jill home with her and kept her the whole time I was in the hospital. My sister Maribelle in Spokane offered to come and take care of us until I felt strong enough to get back to being a mother and housewife again.

Jill and Alton became very close. He taught her the alphabet, and they wrote letters on each other's back, guessing what they were. Since Alan had taken over most of the farm work, Alton had more time to spend with this baby than he'd had with the others. He read to her almost as much as I did in those years before she started school and taught her card games they could play together. I almost felt left out, but the doctor had cautioned me not to lift or carry Jill, and that was the way it had to be. Those first six years went by so fast. I felt I had lost those baby years when a child seems to learn as if by magic.

The winter Jill was seven was a hard winter with lots of snow. The yard was piled high with drifts, and a trip to town was an ordeal. One day in January there was a phone call from school. It was the school principal, and he asked to speak to Alton. "I'll be right there," Alton told him.

All Alton would tell me was that Jill was acting strangely, and he had to go and get her. I didn't know why I was kept in the dark, or why he wouldn't take me with him. In a short time he called and said they were taking Jill to the hospital in Havre. When I called the teacher she was vague and wouldn't tell me much. Apparently they thought they were protecting me from bad news because of my heart, but it was the worst thing they could have done. I was frantic. When I called her teacher again, she told me what had happened.

"Jill just got up from her seat, walked across the room, and stood in the corner with her face to the wall," she said. "She didn't answer when I spoke her name and didn't seem to know where she was. When her friend Nancy went over and led Jill back to her seat, she seemed to be in a hypnotic state. Alton is on the way to the hospital with her now, and he will call us as soon as he can."

I remembered that Elizabeth Patrick had a jeep and called her. She came right out, fighting the snowdrifts, and took me to the hospital in Havre. Alton was still there, and Jill was sitting up in bed when we arrived. Although she looked a little flushed, she seemed all right. The doctor said it was probably the aftermath of a bout of flu Jill had just been through. We accepted his diagnosis and took her home. She didn't seem to be suffering any ill effects, so things were soon back to normal. The next week during her piano lesson her teacher called and said to come and get her right away. Jill was having a seizure.

This time when we rushed her into the hospital the doctor said she probably had a brain tumor. Alton and I clung to each other as the doctor made an appointment with a neurologist in Great Falls. Neither of us slept that night, and it was a long two-hour drive with neither us of wanting to talk. Jill seemed cheerful enough, though, and didn't even seem to mind the tests too much. The results of the encephalogram showed that she had grand mal epilepsy. The doctor prescribed Dilantin and Phenobarbital and suggested we take her to a specialist in Oregon as soon as possible. This specialist was renowned in his field, and after a series of examinations gave us the first good news we'd had. He said that although she did have grand mal epilepsy, there was a very good chance that she could outgrow it and lead a normal life. He said to keep on with the medications.

By the age of ten Jill appeared to have grown out of even the small seizures and was doing well in school. She was still on the medication and insisted that she take it herself. We agreed since she would probably have to take it the rest of her life.

A series of events changed our lives considerably that year. Anna Briedal, whose land Alton had been leasing, decided to sell, and she gave Alton first refusal, with low interest and a very good price. We talked it over with Alan and decided that he should buy her land, since all he had ever wanted to do was farm. Alan fixed up a bunkhouse on the old farmstead separate from the house for himself, complete with bathroom and fireplace, and we were all quite comfortable.

The fall of 1974 Sandra came home to help with harvest and offered to stay a few days with Jill so Alton and I could go on a little trip. I wanted to look for a small piece of land on Flathead Lake where we could put our little trailer so we could go camping once in a while, and Alton agreed but I don't think he had any intention of following through. We phoned a realtor and he halfheartedly showed us several places that we found unsuitable. We went to bed, planning to get an early start home. While Alton was out having coffee the next morning I phoned another realtor, and he said he had a perfect place in mind for us. Alton didn't want to take the time but finally agreed to look at this one more place. It was a blue and gold morning, with the lake sparkling and the spacious yard smelling of new mown grass. There was a plum, a pear, an apricot, and an apple tree in the yard. Chrysanthemums bloomed against a white fence. The house sat on nearly a hundred feet of lakeshore, and the price included a good fishing boat.

"I could live here and be happy the rest of my life," Alton said. Before we left for the farm we had put down a thousand dollars earnest money.

It turned out to be the best decision we ever made. We suffered pangs of buyer's remorse and during those first few days almost decided to forfeit the earnest money and back out, but we kept our bargain and were never sorry that we did. We had so many family get-togethers at the lake house. Jill's wedding and our fiftieth wedding anniversary were both celebrated there.

Jill was thirteen when we moved to Big Arm on Flathead Lake, and she hated the idea of having to move from the farm where she had grown up. She would be leaving all her friends and attending a big school, and there were physical changes that she would have to deal with. She was very unhappy for a while, but then she became friends with a couple of kids down the road and made friends in school and seemed settled and reasonably happy.

Alton was driving back and forth from the farm every week, and Jill and I were doing fine. We had almost forgotten about her epilepsy. Then one day she got off the school bus and I could see that she had been crying. She wouldn't tell me what the trouble was, but a friend told her mother, and she called me. It seemed that the teacher had thought Jill wasn't paying attention and pulled her hair. Jill had been experiencing a petit mal seizure.

I was seething and went over to my neighbor's house to ask if she knew who the teacher was. She told me that she was almost ready to retire and that I should keep that in mind. I phoned the school and told the principal that I was on my way in and wanted to see them both. The teacher was a mulish-looking woman, and although I could see that she had been crying, she wasn't ready to admit that she was in the wrong.

"If you had told us about her epilepsy, this wouldn't have happened," she said.

"Does that mean then that you feel justified in pulling a little girl's hair if she doesn't have epilepsy?" I asked. "Tell me how you think she felt about being humiliated in front of her classmates, because I plan to phone my husband tonight and maybe we'll decide to humiliate you in front of your peers."

The principal interrupted. "But, Mrs. Sterry, you surely don't want to take this teacher's livelihood away because of one mistake."

One mistake? I seriously doubted that a teacher who was soon to retire hadn't pulled a child's hair before, perhaps many times, but after talking to Alton, we settled for an apology to Jill in front of the whole class, without mentioning her epilepsy, and said we would talk it over at home and decide what to do. That was as far as it went. Jill didn't want us to push the matter any further, and Alton said it was best to let it drop. It could turn a bad situation into even more of an embarrassment for Jill.

She began to have seizures several times a week. She would crash like a felled tree, but in minutes would be up and waiting for the bus, and she didn't want any help from me. I'll never know the hurts she suffered. Somehow she kept from having the grand mal attacks when she was with her friends. I think that when she felt it coming on, she would run for the bathroom. Most worrisome was that Jill began to have a terrible personality change. She became a completely different person and acted as though she hated me. I told myself that this was ordinary behavior for a girl her age.

Since Alton was helping out on the farm he didn't see any of this, and so he wasn't too concerned though I tried to tell him how awful it was. She glowered and her voice turned into a deep growl when she spoke to me. Even her looks changed. She had a studio picture taken for school, and her face was twisted in a hateful expression.

It was months before we could get her an appointment with an epilepsy clinic in Seattle, and her condition continued to deteriorate. Leaving her in Seattle at the hospital was one of the hardest things I've ever had to do, but the treatment helped.

When she returned home about three weeks later, she was distant and wary with both Alton and me. Her medicine had been changed, and she was thin and nervous, but things slowly started to improve. She gradually began to live the normal life of a high school sophomore. She was on the drill team, took driver's education, and completed a drive around the lake at night before passing the written exams.

Meanwhile the specialist in Seattle kept in touch. He had written a paper concerning Jill's unusual case, delivered it at a conference in Europe, and wanted to do a follow-up. When she was a junior in college he paid her expenses to come to Seattle and go through a series of tests. She was a little doubtful at first, but finally agreed. He called us after that and said that Jill must have been an exceptionally strong person to have gotten through those years.

Jill went on to finish college and drove by herself to San Francisco to get a job, after which she joined the National Reserves and got through basic training. She later became an occupational therapist's assistant. We worried about her when she was pregnant with her two children, afraid that the stress might set off another spell, but she got through two Cesarean births without extraordinary trauma. Once again we felt blessed.

Going Home

It is December 1996, and it has been a long tiring day. Alton has driven through ice and snow, the big semis throwing slush on our windshield as they pass one after the other. We are headed for Arizona to spend the winter months and have finally reached the small town in Utah where we plan to spend the night. Alton has gone out to find a money machine, and it is now an hour since he left and I'm frantic. I put on my coat and start walking up the street.

There he is, driving back and forth. He doesn't see me when I wave. I walk out in the middle of the street, and still he doesn't see me. I take off my coat and wave it, and then he stops. He is white and shaky and won't talk to me. Now I'm scared and go to the office to call Craig. There is nothing he can do, but I have to talk to someone. I promise to call him the next day.

Alton seems like his old self in the morning, but very quiet. The rest of the trip he hardly talks at all and driving through the Phoenix traffic tires him more than usual.

He is restless this winter and has sudden bursts of temper over little things like missing a green light or losing his comb. When I am addressing Christmas cards he can't find his aunt's name and throws my address book outside. He doesn't want to play bridge with me or go to any of the functions provided for the villagers at Monte Vista. He begins talking about going home right after New Year's. I think he is joking at first, but he really means it.

He agrees to be my partner at the Friday night duplicate bridge club after I coax and coax. We are all in the card room waiting to start when he comes in with blood streaming down from one ear. He has tripped on a rock and fallen, he says. I go with him to the emergency room, and after a long wait they start to sew up the cuts on his ear. I think briefly that he might have had a stroke and ask if he shouldn't be x-rayed, but the doctor is overtired and Alton protests vehemently, so he is discharged. It is only a fifteen-minute drive from the hospital to Monte Vista, but he gets lost and it takes us another hour to get home.

And still I don't suspect that there is anything seriously wrong. Then when I see that he is losing weight, I try to get him to go to a doctor.

"I'm alright," he snaps. "For God's sake just leave me alone!" I back off, but I still worry.

Rick calls one day and says he wants to come for a visit in February. The night he arrives we linger at the table after supper, and I can't believe what I am hearing. Alton is talking about plans for his last rites. "I know most of my friends are gone now," he says, "but I have three sons and three grandsons to serve as pallbearers." When I have tried to talk about our final plans before this he has refused to discuss it.

Sensing that they want to be alone, I go to bed, and they stay up long after midnight. I can't sleep.

"I didn't realize how hard I was making you work all those years," I hear Alton say. "I guess I stole a lot of your boyhood. God, but I'm sorry. I'm sorry about so many things. I was always so proud of you. Why didn't I tell you that?"

"All the farm kids worked hard," Rick tells him, denying that he had ever felt overworked. "That was the way of life then," he says. "We all worked."

They do a lot of hugging that night, maybe to make up for the hug-less years.

After Rick's visit Alton seems almost jaunty, going on long runs around the park, and even consenting to play bridge with me once in a while. It is as though a heavy burden has been lifted from his shoulders.

Our trip home in March is scary. Alton still won't let me drive, even when the roads are good. He says he's going to take the shortcut around by West Yellowstone, and I threaten to catch a ride with a stranger if he takes that perilous route. He pulls over and looks so white and tired that I beg him to let me drive this time. When he refuses I give him a neck and back massage at the next rest stop. We stop overnight at Jill and her husband Jerry's place west of Livingston, mainly to see our granddaughter, Halsey. Jill is seven months pregnant and not feeling very well with this pregnancy.

Alton is agitated and asks the same questions over and over. He has been doing that for a while, but not as much as this day. I want to stay another night, but he is adamant, so we leave. I ask him to stop for a cup of coffee in Dunkirk, and he says he's never heard of such a place, but he does turn in, and then declares he's never been there in his life. I tell myself that he's just trying to start an argument, so I let it go.

We arrive home that Monday night, and Alton goes to town the next day to pick up the mail and get some groceries. I don't see any change in him except that he complains of his shoulder hurting from his fall and has me call the doctor for an appointment on Thursday morning.

Rick phones to say he and Quince, his second son, are driving out for a ski trip. They will be joining his other son, Sky, in Bozeman, and plan to stop at the lake on Sunday and to spend the night with us. Alan will be coming over from the farm. Alton is excited that his sons and grandson are coming. Every half hour he asks if Rick shouldn't be arriving pretty soon.

"He isn't coming until Sunday," I say, "and this is only Thursday."

"Oh, that's right," he says, and then asks the same question just a few minutes later.

I am brushing my teeth and getting ready for bed when Alton calls me. "Look," he says. "That picture is just like the one we have at the lake."

I don't see anything unusual. "What picture are you talking about?" I ask.

"That picture on the wall, the one with the oranges. It's just like the one we have at home."

I know then that we're in trouble. "But we are home," I say. "No, we're not, not yet," he says.

I have gone with Alton to see the doctor. "He's okay," the doctor says. "He'll be his old self again with a few days' rest."

Twice, driving home from Polson after the doctor's appointment, he almost hits a logging truck. "Pull over, pull over!" I scream, but he doesn't seem to hear me. As soon as we get home, he goes out to the garage and starts looking through the cupboards, making piles of tools and odds and ends. I ask him what he's looking for.

"I'm looking for my stuff . . . it's my stuff, isn't it," he says.

This is only Thursday, and the boys will not arrive until Sunday. I think of Alzheimer's, and I think of a stroke. I try to call the doctor, but he is out of town. I call the hospital, and they say they can't admit Alton without doctor's orders. Mostly, I just follow Alton around.

It is still cold in March, and Alton keeps going outside to the boathouse and the garage without a coat. He searches all over the house and piles our passports on the table along with other small belongings: the key to the bank vault, his checkbook, and wallet. "We'll need these where we're going," he says. I ask him where we are going. "We're going home. We're going home, of course," he says with a smile.

I call Jill and she advises me to hide the keys to the vehicles. I wrap them in a scarf and put them in the corner of the organ bench. He never looks there. Alan arrives mid-afternoon and is shocked when he sees his dad. Alton has become a frail old man in just these three days. It's as though the aging process has been set on fast forward. He stoops and shuffles when he walks. His eyes seem sunken, his cheeks hollow, and he is so thin. I want to put my arms around him and hold him like a baby. When I reach to touch him he backs away.

He goes outside again with Alan after him, and then Alan comes in with the keys for the car and pickup in his hand. "Dad gave them to me," he says. I have been here all the time, and I never saw him near the organ bench where I had hidden them. Alan goes out and brings his dad in again, challenging him to a game of cribbage. They are still playing, with Alan losing badly, when Rick and Quince arrive. I see how stunned they are when they see Alton. He is so glad to see them that he almost seems normal. I haven't slept for two nights, and I gladly let Rick take over. I have a roast in the oven, and the boys play pool with Alton while I get supper on the table.

The phrase "pull yourself together" is demonstrated more than once that night. Alton looks bewildered, and then he makes a mighty effort and literally pulls his mind and soul together. "Come and see the Hale-Bopp Comet, Grandpa," Quince says, and we all go out on the deck. There it is, unbelievably big and bright and awesome as it moves across the sky. Alton is hanging in there, but Rick and Quince have driven all the way from Eugene and we are exhausted. We decide to talk the situation over in the morning.

We finally get to sleep and I wake up to find Alton standing beside the bed. He is looking for a clean pair of pajamas, and he is white and shaky. He is cold when I put my arms around him to lead him back to bed. "Go back to sleep, honey," I say. I am so tired. I go right to sleep.

I feel a hand on my shoulder. Someone is shaking me. "What is it, Alton?" I say.

"No, it's Rick. Wake up, Mom. Wake up! Dad has fallen down the stairs."

"Is it bad?" I say

"Yes, it's bad," he says. I reach for my robe. I want to go to him. "No, Mom, no," Rick says. "You shouldn't go down there." I try to go downstairs, but Alan blocks my way.

"No, Mom," he says.

Rick calls 911. Quince goes out to stand by the road with a flashlight to signal the ambulance.

Alan won't let me go downstairs to see Alton or ride with him in the ambulance. I ride with Rick, trailing the comet all the way. When we get to the hospital in Polson I hear Alton moaning, and know he's in terrible pain, but the doctor says he can't feel anything. I know he's lying. They are sending him to Missoula in a helicopter. We take Alan with us and drive to the hospital in Missoula, seventy-five miles away, and then wait and wait until the doctor, an infinitely kind man, comes to talk to us.

"It's just a matter of time," he tells us.

Rick puts his arm around me. "How much time?" he asks.

"Twelve hours at most," the doctor tells him. "You can see him now."

Rick looks at me and I nod my head very carefully, because it is full of glass marbles that shift from side to side when I move. We walk behind the doctor down that long white hall. There is a whistling in my ears, and I hear people crying and then see that it is us. The doctor opens a door and steps aside to let me go in first. I can't take that first step, and then something or someone takes my hand, and I am standing by his bed. This is not Alton. I kiss his face, and it is like kissing a stone.

I hold his hands, his beautiful hands, but they are icy. His heart is beating, but no one is there. It is as though he is frozen in a block of ice. I want to say goodbye. I want to touch him, but there is a chasm between us that I can't reach across.

He has gone ahead without me.

We eat something someplace, maybe the hospital cafeteria.

"You all are suffering so," the kind doctor tells us when we come back. "You need to get some rest. Maybe we should turn the machine off and let Alton go."

Everyone is absorbed in his own personal grief, and I know I have to decide. "Yes," I say.

We began the interminable phone calls. Sandra, Max, Craig, John, and Sophie start right out from their home in Oregon. Jill drives over from Livingston, and soon I am surrounded by my children. Quince takes Rick's car and goes to Bozeman to get Sky.

We drive back to our home on the lake, Alan, Rick, and I. It is a grief-filled trip home that afternoon, and I'm not finished yet. I telephone Sharon Spicher in Hingham, and although she is inundated by Easter plans, she helps me with the funeral arrangements. The phone rings and rings, and I try to answer.

"Mom," Alan says. "I can't bear to hear you tell that story one more time today. Just don't answer any more."

Alan and Rick have spent the afternoon helping each other through this and supporting me in my grief. Jill is only about six weeks from delivery, and she is trying hard not to let her grief hurt the baby. The Oregon family drives in wearing their agony and their fear. Our feelings are too deep to help each other. I go lie down for a small nap. I sleep through dinner.

When we arrive at the farm the next day the Spichers have brought their trailer out for the overflow of family. Friends have cleaned the house and the oven, and the refrigerator is full of food. That's the way it's done where we come from. Jerry, Jill's husband, drives over with Halsey, and Alton has his wish. His three sons and his three grandsons are his pallbearers.

The funeral, the memorial service, is like a dream. Craig, Sandra, Rick, and Alan do all the many things that need to be done, and I go back to Eugene with Sandra. It isn't a good idea. They all have their own grief to bear, and I am alone in a strange place. I am relieved when Sandra drives me back to the lake. I can see that I will not be able to keep up with the yard work and solve the many little glitches in running things that only Alton knew about. I sell our lovely place on the lake and buy a house in town. This lake, these strong mountains. It is finished, and I must start a new life, a new life without the other half of me.

My friend Sylvia carries out the last of the boxes filled with cards and pictures. I can't bear to throw any of them away. I walk through the house one last time. I go out to the boathouse and climb into the boat that Alton was so proud of. I walk along the shore, go through the garden, inspect the roses. Everything is beginning to look shabby without him. I start to go in the door downstairs but I can't walk by that spot, that place where his broken body had been. I turn and go back up the outside steps, look for my purse, and then I hear a bell chime, over and over, a single chime.

"Come on," Sylvia says. "It's the doorbell . . . only the doorbell."

But my doorbell has a double ring, and I know it is Alton saying goodbye.

Family Tree

Adelia Frances Hamilton m. William Hanson
b. 1883-d. 19 | b. 1883-d. 1958

Irene
b. 1912-d. 1989

Maribelle   Maggie Amdahl m. Olaf Sterry
b. 1914-d. 1991   b. 1872-d. 1965 | b. 1873?-d. 1956

Willard (Billy)   Norman
b. 1916   b. 1910-d. 1999

Nedra ———— m. ———— Alton
b-1918   b. 1913-d. 1997

Donna   Bernice
b. 1921-d. 1985   b. 1915

Betty Lou   Margie
b. 1922   b. 1919-d. 1984

Harriet   Delos
b. 1923-d. 1988   b. 1921-d. 1971

Rick
b. 1938

Craig
b. 1943

Alan
b. 1944

Sandra
b. 1947

Jill
b. 1961

About the Author

Nedra Sterry has published pieces in the *Great Falls Tribune* Sunday Supplement and *Rural Life*. She is presently working on a book about her husband's aunt, who homesteaded in North Dakota in 1902. She lives in Portland, Oregon.